# BROUGHTON

## From Wellington to Airbus

*Paul McKinlay, Airbus Broughton Head of Plant.*

'We've invested £1.8bn here over the past ten years on the back of tremendous product peformance and great success in the market place'. *Liverpool Daily Post*

*The Broughton Wellington: The Vickers Wellington Mk.IC R1333 Second World War bomber that was subscribed by the 'Workers and Co-operators' of the Vickers-Chester Shadow Factory built in 1939 at the Flintshire, North Wales, village of Broughton, near Chester, and ceremoniously presented to the Royal Air Force in November 1940. Wellington production there totalled 5,540 aircraft in the six years between August 1939 and July 1944 and peaked at 130 aircraft per month. Interestingly, this total was approximately equivalent to one complete aircraft for each member of the workforce at its peak.*

*The patriarchal Airbus A300B airliner prototype/demonstrator – the world's first twin-aisle twin-engined jet airliner – which heralded the inauguration of a dynasty that would go on to transform the Airbus consortium, formally constituted on 18 December 1970, into the world-leading large transport aircraft manufacturer that it is today. Incorporating Chester/Broughton-built wings and registered F-WUAB, this seminal and innovative new European airliner concept demonstrator made its maiden flight at Toulouse in Southern France on 28 October 1972. Later re-registered as F-OCAZ, it made extensive development and sales tours before achieving certification on 15 March 1974 – prefacing entry-into-service with launch customer, Air France, on 23 May 1974 on the London-Paris route. It proved to be the harbinger from which Airbus was to progress from a one-product organization into that which now, 40 years later, is promoting a comprehensive globally-appealing fourteen-member commercial airliner, corporate business, and military transport and aerial refuelling tanker aircraft family. All incorporate Chester/Broughton-built wings and craftsmanship. More than 8,500 sets of wings have now been completed at this uniquely-productive aerostructures factory and Airbus has amassed a total order book of more than 14,000 aircraft.*

# BROUGHTON

## From Wellington to Airbus

NORMAN BARFIELD

*Dedicated to those many thousands whose exceptional efforts over the past seven decades have built
the Broughton Factory into the world-class aerostructures manufacturing facility that it is today.*

Front cover illustration: *In the foreground, the third development new generation Airbus A350XWB (eXtra Wide Body) mid-size, long-range and highly fuel-, eco- and operating cost-efficient airliner, liveried to symbolise the dominant content of non-metallic carbon-fibre content of the airframe structure. In the background, the fourth development aircraft hybrid-liveried in the colours of Airbus and Qatar Airways of Doha, the A350XWB family launch customer. Together they highlight the aerodynamically advanced Airbus Broughton-built carbon-fibre wing structures, the newest of more than 8,500 Airbus airliner family wing sets built at the historic Broughton factory during the past 45 years. After the initiating production of 5,540 wartime Vickers Wellington bombers between 1939 to 1944, a further 4,132 Avro, de Havilland, Hawker Siddeley and British Aerospace 'fly-away' aircraft were also built there between 1994 and 1996 – making it one of the most accomplished aircraft manufacturing plants anywhere in the world.*

Back cover illustration: *The view of the now huge Airbus Broughton factory complex was taken across the wing of the Airbus A380 double-deck intercontinental airliner by a crew member during its UK 'show-the-workforce' debut on 18 May 2006, and for which the world's largest airliner wing was built there in the purpose-built 'West Factory' located under the wing root in the foreground of the picure. The newly-constructed, also purpose-built, 'North Factory' for the assembly of the 'majority carbon-fibre' wing structure for the next generation A350XWB is now located under the wing tip. Seen in the centre is the cavernous Airbus A300–600ST 'Beluga' outsize freighter aircraft at the load-out area of the 'East Factory' and used on a daily basis for the distinctive Airbus 'wings-on-wings' transport for the A320, A330 and A350XWB families to their continental European equipping and aircarft final assembley centre in Bremen and Hamburg, Germany and Toulouse, France. The core structure of this latter Broughton factory unit (with the surviving externally-evident 'Northern Light' 'high' main assembly area seen in the centre – and in construction on p. 33) constituted the original Second World War Vickers–Chester 'Shadow Factory'.*

First published in 2001 by Tempus Publishing
Reprinted 2002
This edition 2007
Reprinted in 2011

This edition printed in 2014

The History Press
The Mill, Brimscombe Port,
Stroud, Gloucestershire, GL5 2QG
www.thehistorypress.co.uk

British Library Cataloguing in Publication Data.
A catalogue record for this book is available from the British Library.

ISBN 978 0 7524 4184 9

Printed and bound in Great Britain by Marston Book Services Limited, Oxfordshire.

# Contents

# The Shadow Factory Scheme

The rise to power of Adolf Hitler, with his accession to the German Chancellery in 1933 and his repudiation of the terms of the Versailles Treaty of 1919, resulted in the British Government abandoning its belief that disarmament was the road to peace. They had to face the reality that Germany was building up its arsenal in readiness for another war.

The situation quickly came to a head at the League of Nations Disarmament Conference of October 1933, Geneva, when the German delegation precipitously walked out. Despite great efforts to revive it, their action ultimately resulted in the Conference being abandoned in June 1934.

The evident alarm this caused, together with widespread rumours of greatly increased military aircraft production in Germany, led the British Prime Minister, Stanley Baldwin, to announce a substantial Expansion Programme for the Royal Air Force on 19 July 1934. The primary objective was to increase aircraft production in order to achieve parity with the German *Luftwaffe* by no later than April 1939.

At the same time, the aircraft industry was introducing radical changes in design – more powerful engines and more potent armaments – and grappling with the increased time taken to ready these new types for operational service. The manufacturing capacity of the industry was grossly insufficient to meet the perceived needs of the RAF and therefore required a correspondingly radical solution.

So it was that the Government conceived the 'Shadow Factory Scheme'. This consisted principally of utilizing related manufacturing capacity outside the aircraft and aero-engine industries. Primarily, it included the expanding motor vehicle industry, which was by then the national leader in large-scale mechanical engineering, metallic fabrication and mass production techniques, with the major motor manufacturers 'shadowing' the professional aviation industry.

The function of these additional factories would be to produce in quantity any type of airframe or engine that had been officially frozen in design. This, in turn, would allow the parent firms to develop new or improved types and, in reasonable time, to establish large-scale production at the shadow factories, enabling production to keep abreast of operational requirements.

Accordingly, the Air Ministry invited six major motor manufacturers to participate. The Government funded the new factories but the firms themselves supervised the construction and management, including the recruitment and training of the necessary labour force.

The locational criteria were that the factories should be near to populous areas from which the requisite labour force could be drawn, have ease of road and rail access, and be on or near existing aerodromes to facilitate flight testing and delivery (or, if not, to include the construction of a new one). They should be geographically dispersed to prevent stoppage in the event of a successful enemy air attack on one of them and hence be situated out of range of enemy bombers where possible.

Several such large units were thus established in the Midlands and the north-west of England, but away from the well-established aircraft factories with locations, mainly in the South, which were well known to the enemy, and most of them were managed by the motor industry. However, those for the Vickers Wellington bomber were not. The project had been seriously considered at the big Nuffield plant at Castle Bromwich, Birmingham but, in the event, Spitfire fighters were built there instead, also under the aegis of Vickers.

Vickers-Armstrongs had planned a large dispersal factory of its own for the Wellington at Broughton, near Chester – the site of which, and its subsequent story to date, is the subject of this book (together with a second autonomous plant near Blackpool which is also included here as a directly related cameo). Both plants ultimately became Government-owned, Vickers-managed, units within the Shadow Factory Scheme.

# Introduction

Seventy-five years on from the establishment in September 1939 of its original being as a Second World War 'Shadow Factory' for large-scale production of the Vickers Wellington geodetic ('basketweave') bomber – one of the few aircraft types that continued in production throughout the conflict – and 45 years on from the launch of the pan-European Airbus Industrie (AI) airliner manufacturing programme on 29 May 1969, what is today the Airbus UK Factory at Broughton, Flintshire, North Wales, is the exclusive Airbus manufacturing plant for the wing structures of the complete range of the globally successful Airbus commercial airliner family. Consistently Britain's largest and most productive aircraft factory since its inception, Broughton today produces a far greater tonnage of aerostructures than the rest of the British industry combined and is widely acclaimed as one of the most productive and efficient aerostructures manufacturing plants anywhere in the world.

Passing successively from Vickers-Armstrongs to de Havilland, Hawker Siddeley, British Aerospace, BAE Systems, EADS Airbus UK, and now the Airbus Group in the UK, this huge facility has delivered nearly 9,700 'fly-away' military and civil aircraft of fifteen different types. They range from the famed Wellington and Lancaster bombers of Second World War vintage, though to the world-leading Comet jetliner and 125 business jet. The factory has produced more than 8,500 sets of Airbus airliner wings during the second half of this time period: an overall production record unparalleled by any other British aircraft factory.

Although never having had an autonomous corporate identity of its own, the Broughton Factory's exceptional production record and provenance have meant that it has gained global influence and a reputation equivalent to that of the founding British aircraft firms that featured so strongly in its early years.

---

### 75 YEARS ON
#### 2014 – A VINTAGE YEAR FOR AIRBUS BROUGHTON

Five significant events are being celebrated at Broughton this year which effectively embrace the entire history and outstanding achievements of what is today one of the most advanced and accomplished aerospace factories in the world:

- Seventy-fifth Anniversary of its original establishment in September 1939 as a Second World War 'Shadow Factory' for large-scale manufacture of Vickers Wellington and Avro Lancaster bombers.

- Forty-fifth Anniversary of the formal establishment of the Airbus Industrie airliner programme on 29 May 1969.

- Fortieth Anniversary of the introduction into service of the first production Broughton-built Airbus A300 airliner with Air France on the London–Paris route on 23 May 1974.

- Broughton became part of the newly re-branded Airbus Group (superseding the former European Aeronautics and Space (EADS) on 1 January 2014.

- Queen's Award for Enterprise accorded to Airbus in the UK in April 2014 'for international trade for outstanding overseas sales over the last three year'.

---

*Erection of the steelwork of the main factory area which, when completed in September 1939, was traversed throughout the uninterrupted roof girders by a unique and powerful overhead rapid-transit crane system.*

Beginning essentially as a complete aircraft assembly plant for the Wellington, although much component and detail support work has also been progressively inducted into the Broughton plant over the years, it has always relied heavily on external supply. In the Vickers years, this consisted of an exclusive network of 500 suppliers mainly in the north-west and Midlands (and from the several Avro wartime plants in the Manchester area for the Lancaster). During the de Havilland era, major components were imported from the DH sites at Hatfield, Portsmouth, Christchurch, and Downsview, Canada; also from Fairey Aviation at Stockport and Saunders Roe at Eastleigh, Southampton and Cowes, Isle of Wight. In the Hawker Siddeley and British Aerospace years, this circle was widened even further to include Woodford and Chaddereton (near Manchester), Brough, (Yorkshire) and Hamble (near Southampton).

The massive subsequent build-up of Airbus wing construction in the British Aerospace/BAE Systems and Airbus UK regimes has progressively embraced many other UK and overseas sources, notably including Weybridge, Filton, Prestwick, Samlesbury, Australia, Korea, Malaysia, Sweden and the USA, and 400 other suppliers throughout the UK – with Broughton itself simultaneously becoming essentially a major component supplier to the continental-based Airbus final assembly centres at Toulouse in Southern France and Finkenwerder, near Hamburg, in Germany.

Now effectively doubled in size and capacity, fully modernised to cater for the A380 'Super Jumbo', and advancing into the twenty-first century in its vital wing manufacturing 'Centre of Excellence' role in fulfilling the burgeoning global Airbus airliner order book and its continually expanding family lineage and delivering around 600 wing sets per year, the Airbus UK Broughton Factory and its 6,500-strong workforce is not only the pride of British aerostructures manufacture but also an acknowledged model of quality, efficiency and standard-setting for the rest of the aerospace world.

# Genesis

A critical time in the history of Europe was in 1932 when Germany left the Disarmament Conference and shortly afterwards announced its intention of building up an Air Force which had been banned under the 1919 Treaty of Versailles. Great strides were made in this direction during the next few years and by 1935 it was apparent to all that Germany was determined to achieve aerial supremacy. Consequently anticipating the very real threat of another major conflict looming in Europe, in 1935 the British Government introduced a major 'Expansion Scheme' for the Royal Air Force.

Late in 1934, the Air Ministry had also asked Vickers to consider a scheme for the complete removal of its Weybridge, Surrey, and Southampton (Supermarine) aircraft plants, both dangerously near possible hostile air bases on the continent, to safer areas in the North and out-of-reach of potential enemy bombing attacks. On the recommendation of Commander Sir Charles Craven, then Managing Director, Works and Shipyards, of Vickers-Armstrongs Ltd, a large area at Flookburgh

*The original Vickers-Armstrongs wartime Shadow Factory and Royal Air Force Aerodrome, as they appeared on completion in September 1939 (but with the five small hangars in the foreground added early in the de Havilland tenure), facing the Hawarden Aerodrome main runway in a north-easterly direction. This completely new Wellington bomber assembly production facility was completed and operational in only nine months from the initial ground-breaking in mid-December 1938.*

near the company's shipyard at Barrow-in-Furness, Cumbria, was chosen as a site for a combined facility, but the proposal had to be abandoned as soon as the Expansion Scheme was instigated as the move would have held up production of urgently needed aircraft for some considerable time.

In reality, when both original factories were bombed within two days of each other (4 and 6 September 1940 respectively) they were widely dispersed in their local areas before becoming fully operational again. Continuing to develop successive new variants of their mainstream products – the Wellington bomber and Spitfire fighter respectively – the huge quantity production requirements were to be handled by wholly new 'Shadow Factories' where established aircraft types could be made, either by existing aircraft firms or by companies from other industries that had experience of 'mass-production assembly line' production. For the Vickers types, these were located at Chester and Blackpool for the Wellington, and at Castle Bromwich (near Birmingham) for the Spitfire.

When preparations were being made to put the new Vickers Wellington into full-scale production, after the aircraft had first flown in prototype form on 15 June 1936 at the company's headquarters plant at Weybridge, it was realised that the factory facilities there would not be able to cope alone with the anticipated large initiating orders for the re-designed production version.

Accordingly, Sir Robert McLean, the forceful Chairman of Vickers (Aviation) Ltd, approached the British Government with plans for an additional £1 million factory, with a potential output of 50 per cent higher than the originating Vickers-Weybridge plant, and a decision to build a new plant was taken three months later in September of that year. Unlike Weybridge, it was to be an assembly works only, with all component and sub-assemblies subcontracted, and hence to be entirely independent of the operations at Weybridge so that production and the development of new versions there could continue uninterrupted. However, the actual construction did not begin until December 1938.

Gordon ('Monty') Montgomery was a Vickers-Weybridge veteran, a contemporary of Tommy Sopwith at Brooklands and a member of the Royal Flying Corps. He had notably led the team that assembled the historic Alcock and Brown Vickers Vimy of transatlantic fame in Newfoundland in 1919 and supervised the building of the Vickers B.9/32 Wellington prototype in 1936 and the Wellesleys of the RAF's record-breaking Egypt-Australia Long Range Flight in 1938. Towards the end of 1937, Montgomery had ostensibly taken his family on holiday in North Wales and Scotland. The real reason for these excursions, however, was to assess the options of building a Wellington Shadow Factory near Chester, in the north-west of England or in Inverness, Scotland. In the event,

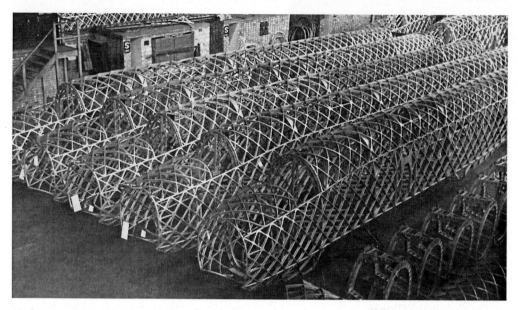

*The unique and distinctive geodetic ('basketweave') structure of the Wellington airframe: 8,946 of these aircraft were built at the Vickers-Chester and -Blackpool shadow factories (5,540 and 3,406 respectively) during the Second World War.*

the former was chosen because the latter was considered too remote and subject to unacceptable weather conditions for continuous winter operations. The Chester site was one of the few areas in North Wales that could accommodate an airfield with a reasonably clear year-round test flying area.

Alan Cobham's National Aviation Day displays had been flown from an airfield alongside what became the Hawarden Airfield in 1933, and part of the site had been used as a Relief Landing Ground (RLG) by No.5 Flying Training School from the nearby RAF station Sealand. The RLG was known as Bowers Landing Ground, taking its name from Bowers Farm. The Air Ministry's knowledge of the area thus led to the selection of land near the villages of Bretton and the slightly larger Broughton being approved for construction of the new factory, with the adjacent airfield incorporating the former Bowers farm site. The selection was made in November 1937. Whereas most of the shadow factories were managed by the motor industry, the Vickers Wellington plant was not, in the event built under the motor industry scheme. The initial intention was that Vickers-Armstrongs would build and own the factory, but by October 1938 it had been decided that the Air Ministry would finance the building of the plant as a Government-owned Shadow Factory but that it be leased to, and managed by, the company as an agent, sharing the adjacent Hawarden Aerodrome with the Royal Air Force, and for it to be known as 'Vickers-Armstrongs Chester'.

# Building a Big Bomber Birthplace

The intention was that the new factory would be a 'parent works' – i.e. planned as a huge mass production plant only, laid out and built on the concept that the manufacture of all components would be subcontracted – a method which was considered eminently suitable for such an aircraft as the Wellington. This was quite different from Weybridge, where aircraft were built complete, from raw material to the finished product. The same concept applied to the second Vickers-managed Wellington Shadow Factory at Blackpool on the Fylde coast of Lancashire which was, in many respects, a modernised duplicate of Weybridge.

*Wellington production at the Vickers-Chester Shadow Factory.*

As designed, the Chester Factory had no 'back shops', such as fitting, machining etc., other than millwrights. Initially, there were no finished parts stores and it was intended that co-ordinated stocks would be delivered on a daily basis directly to the production line (an early example of the modern-day 'just-in-time' and 'line-side supply' practices). However, the plant did not continue in this fashion. As the tempo of production built up, large stocks of parts did have to be accommodated on and off site.

Ground-breaking construction work began on 14 December 1938, the civil engineering contractor being the famed Sir William Arrol and Son of Clydeside, Scotland. The builders of Tower Bridge and the Forth Bridge, and in 1926 they had also constructed the nearby Queensferry Bridge which spanned the River Dee to the Wirral peninsular, traversed daily by many of the factory employees over the past 60-odd years. Though long dormant, the company is still registered in the portfolio of Langley Holdings at Retford, Nottinghamshire. The completed factory became fully operational in September 1939. The distinctive feature of the layout was the huge open aircraft assembly area, some 1,200ft long, with annexed side bays for the feed-in of component assemblies and dressed engines, and at the end of which was a clear uninterrupted roof area of 650ft square. This gave it the largest single-span roof area of any aircraft factory in Europe at that time – 1.5 million sq.ft with a main assembly area of around 1 million sq.ft.

Adjoining land was purchased by the Air Ministry during construction from the Hawarden Estate, where the supporting aerodrome was built – originally for the RAF – by Bernard Sunley and Co., who designed the Birmingham Elmdon Airport amongst others (and still operating today as Sunley Holdings).

# What's in a Name?

At this point, it is necessary to clarify the sometimes-confusing matter of the name of the factory. Initially known by Vickers internally simply as the 'Northern Factory', it was predominantly known throughout most of its life as 'Chester' as originally designated, and because of the historic Roman-walled city four miles to the east in the English county of Cheshire being the nearest well-known landmark. The actual geographical location is on the outskirts of the village of Broughton (pronounced 'Brawton'), about 3½ miles to the south-west of Chester; it is, in fact a mile inside the Welsh border in the county of Flintshire. Hence, it is by this latter name that the factory has often also been known, especially locally. To add to this confusion, it has also been known as

*The Broughton/Hawarden Shadow Factory/RAF Aerodrome complex in the later stages of the Second World War with large numbers of Vickers Wellington and Avro Lancaster bombers awaiting delivery.*

'Hawarden' (pronounced 'Harden'), the name of the better-known small town from which the original supporting RAF aerodrome took its name.

It is now the policy of Airbus UK to use the name 'Broughton' exclusively. This is principally in deference to the recent Welsh political devolution, it being the only aircraft manufacturing facility in Wales (and around 60 per cent of the workforce traditionally being Welsh). All three names appear in this book as applicable in their relevant contexts, time periods and usage.

# The Vickers Bastion of Big Bomber Production

The initial order for 180 Wellingtons was placed with Vickers-Weybridge in August 1936 (only two months after the prototype first flight). In October 1937, prior to setting up the Chester Factory, a contract for 100 Bristol Pegasus-engined Mk.Is was assigned to the Gloster Aircraft Company. These were to be followed by a second batch of 100 of the projected Rolls-Royce Merlin-engined Mk. II. and Glosters was to build the Hawker Hurricane fighter and the Vickers Wellington bomber in parallel. However, by early 1939, when the Chester Factory was nearing completion, and a further contract for 750 aircraft was placed with Vickers on 18 May of that year, it was clear that Glosters could not build both types and certainly not the Wellington at the rate that Chester would be able to do. The Gloster contracts were therefore rescinded by the Government and all raw materials, finished and unfinished parts, and subcontractor chain were transferred to the new plant, thereby enabling Glosters to concentrate solely on large-scale production of the equally urgent Hurricane. Some time later, an order for 64 Wellingtons that had originally been placed with Sir W.G. Armstrong Whitworth Aircraft of Coventry, was also transferred to the Vickers-Blackpool Factory.

Preparations were being made by de Havilland in 1940 for the Mosquito to replace the Airspeed Oxford in production at its parent plant at Hatfield, Hertfordshire. As the Mosquito was not yet a certainty, de Havilland was also approached by the Air Ministry later that year to take on the building of the Vickers Wellington, rising to a rate of 300 units per month, and this they agreed to do.

*Large-scale construction of pre-fabricated aluminium houses for which both the Chester and Blackpool factories were adapted at the end of the Second World War in 1945. Together they produced 22,500 of these ingenious constructions during the ensuing three years.*

As with the Vickers shadow factories at Chester and Blackpool, this involved finding a suitable site with airfield supporting labour, and subcontractors. Although the Wellington option did not materialise, this is how the 'London Production Group', centred at Leavesden, near Watford, originated.

Gordon Montgomery was given the daunting job of assembly manager to get the Chester Wellington production started from scratch.. Having been closely involved in making the Meccano-like geodetic construction a practical proposition at Weybridge, only twenty-two key experienced 'leading hands' were transferred with him. Together, they began to construct the first aircraft on 3 April 1939, in a temporary Bellman-type hangar on the edge of the site near the Glynne Arms public house, while the main factory was being built. Using parts supplied by Weybridge and various subcontractors, this first Chester-built machine, a Wellington Mk.I L7770, was completed four months later and first flown on 2 August 1939. Leaving the Hawarden Airfield initially for Weybridge for production testing, it was delivered to No.99 Squadron RAF in early September, just as the Second World War was starting. The new factory became fully operational, working on what was then known as the 'assembly unit' (AU) system, in September 1939, only nine months from the start of construction, and by the end of December 1939 five aircraft had been completed. Although local subcontractors supplied most of the parts, as intended, there was still considerable reliance on support from Weybridge. By the first anniversary of the start of production, twenty-one aircraft had been built – a remarkable achievement as 98 per cent of the work-force were still only semi-skilled.

Thereafter, expansion was very rapid. Taking the monthly average output per quarter, by the beginning of 1941 Chester was already ahead of Weybridge and by the autumn of 1942 production at Chester was as great as the combined output of Weybridge and Blackpool (which had come 'on-line' in 1940). If production at Chester and Blackpool outran Weybridge, this was, of course, because these two shadow factories were so much larger and they had the Weybridge experience to build on. Weybridge was also deeply committed to the vital spares programme and by the end of 1944 had produced some £28 million worth of Wellington spares.

During 1939, a network of more than 500 subcontractors was established in the north-west of England to supply Wellington parts to the Chester Factory. Typical of these was Anchor Motors in Chester which was the major source of tail unit assemblies, but the network was spread far and wide, with Folland Aircraft at Hamble, near Southampton, also being a major supplier. Significant work had, in fact, already been underway at Gloster Aircraft, such that, when their 'work-in-progress' on tooling and components, and their subcontractors, were transferred to Chester, this greatly aided getting the production moving.

*Large-scale production of the de Havilland Dove and Heron light transports, Vampire and Venom jet fighters, and Comet jet airliners in the early 1950s.*

Paralleling the rapid progress in aircraft delivery was the corresponding build-up of the workforce. On 1 January 1940, there were only 697 workpeople but by the end of September 1943 this number had increased to 5,546 with a further 1,500 on the staff. Significantly, 68 per cent of the assembly workers were women and at the peak of production the head foreman in the final assembly area was a young woman. This was largely because the construction of the fabric covering of the Wellington airframe was akin to tailoring and therefore represented a major contribution for which female labour was regarded to be ideally suited.

As production progressed, the Air Ministry decided to purchase additional land from the Hawarden Estate (of Hawarden Castle, the original home of British Prime Minister, William Gladstone), enabling enlargement of the aerodrome and the establishment of an Aircraft Storage Unit on the northern and western sides of the site (operated later as No.48 Maintenance Unit).

The devastating air raid on the geographically vulnerable Vickers-Weybridge Factory on 4 September 1940, and the resulting severe (if commendably brief) disruption of the well-established Wellington production line there, was an early vindication of the Shadow Factory dimension.

Unfortunately, Gordon Montgomery died in 1941, only 46 years old, but not before the Chester production rate had been built up to more than thirty aircraft a week.

To help maintain the overall Wellington production output at the three factories, and as a further precaution against air attacks, it became necessary for each to open a satellite assembly plant – for Weybridge at Royal Windsor Great Park (Smith's Lawn), mainly for experimental and special versions, for Chester at Byley/Cranage and for Blackpool at Stanley Park – and each with its own airfield. Opened in 1941, the Chester satellite assembly line was actually located at Byley, near Middlewich in mid-Cheshire, about twenty-five miles east of the Chester plant. It was some fields away from the Cranage Aerodrome, which was just to the north-east of the flight shed, and only used for the test flying. However, the combined facility was always known as 'Cranage'. The first machine was completed there in September of that year and the unit accounted for approximately one third of the Wellingtons built on the Chester contract after the site became operational in 1941 (although there is no know breakdown between the two plants). Several satellite component assembly and storage units, mostly with twin hangars, were also dispersed around local villages, including Aston Hall, Dobs Hill, Ewloe and Kinnerton.

From the outset, the Chester/Cranage Wellington production grew rapidly, peaking at a monthly output of 130 aircraft, concentrating on bomber and crew training marks, and reaching a combined

*De Havilland Comet jet airliner production in the mid-1950s.*

total of 5,540 aircraft when production ceased with a Wellington T.10 in September 1945. This was only 380 less than the combined total built at Weybridge and Blackpool (5,920). The Chester and Blackpool shadow factories had between them built four times the number built by the long-established parent Vickers Factory at Weybridge (2,514) but both shadow factories had, of course, been purpose-built and laid out more spaciously for high rates of production from the start. Thus the ultimate Wellington production breakdown between the three factories was: Chester/Cranage 48.3 per cent; Blackpool Squires Gate/Stanley Park 29.7 per cent; and Weybridge/Smith's Lawn 21.9 per cent.

Together, these factories sustained Wellington production throughout the war, making it Britain's most prolific two-motor bomber aircraft programme with a total of 11,460 aircraft produced between them. They made the Wellington one of the most successful aircraft programmes ever – and serving in every command of the RAF, except Fighter.

At one time, plans were well advanced for the Vickers Warwick to follow the Wellington into production at Chester, but the prospective contract for 300 Warwick Is did not materialise, despite significant sums of money being spent in preparation. Plans were also made for production of the Vickers Windsor four-engine heavy bomber but these were also abandoned at an even earlier stage.

As the strategy of the Royal Air Force changed to heavy bomber air raids on key German industrial targets, in March 1943, government instructions were received to taper off Wellington production (orders for more than 600 aircraft were cancelled) and for the Vickers-Chester Factory to join the six-company Avro Lancaster Production Group that had been set up along the lines of the Vickers-Supermarine Spitfire Production Group in September 1941 when the group was further expanded (also to include the Vickers-Castle Bromwich Shadow Factory) to meet the massively increased RAF requirements. An order was then placed with Vickers-Armstrongs on 5 April 1943 for 500 Lancaster B.Mk.I four-engined heavy bombers to be built there – whence the radically different Wellington and Lancaster airframe construction processes began to be operated in parallel.

By September 1944, the Lancaster order book at Chester stood at 680 aircraft and a further 840 of an improved type, the Lincoln. However, the end of the war in Europe in May 1945, and in the Far East in August, meant a drastic curtailment. Only 235 Lancasters were actually built there between June 1944 and September 1945, production during which period reached a peak of 36 aircraft per month in March 1945. The aircraft production programme at Chester was ultimately completed after twenty-three Lancasters and eleven Lincolns had been assembled from components transferred

Left: *The production track of the Hawker Siddeley/British Aerospace 125, the world's first and most successful corporate business jet, and the HS Nimrod main fuselage production line in the late 1960s. The 125 genus continues to be produced at Broughton in airframe component kit form for Raytheon Aircraft Co., USA, now known as the Hawker Beechcraft Corporation, who acquired the programme in 1993 after nearly 1000 units had been produced by HSA/BAe since 1962.*

Opposite: *The principal elemental components in the construction of a typical Airbus wing torsion box/integral fuel tank structure, of which more than 5,000 sets (pairs and hence 10,000 individual wings) have been built at Broughton – the exclusive manufacturing centre for Airbus wings since the start of the programme in 1971.*

from the Metropolitan-Vickers Electrical Co. Factory at Trafford Park, Manchester, between 15 June and 13 August 1945 (and generally included in the total Chester output). These last aircraft were subsequently flown to the Sir W. G. Armstrong Whitworth Aircraft at Coventry late in 1946 for operational conversion to Lancaster B. Mk.I F.E. (Far East) standard (as had been the case with around fifty-five of the earlier Chester-built aircraft).

Near to the completion of the final Ministry of Aircraft Production (MAP) orders, the Chester plant began to slow down, facing closure during the latter months of 1945. Fortuitously, however, an unexpected and substantial new work programme was to materialise just in time to avert this potentially serious eventuality – the construction of 11, 250 prefabricated domestic dwellings.

After the war, the Byley works were retained by the Ministry of Supply as a storage unit and in 1958 the former Vickers paint shop was seen to be accommodating a large range of Avro Anson jigs, incomplete Avro Tudor components and the singular Cierva Air Horse giant helicopter, all up for auction.

# The Blackpool Sibling

Although not directly part of the subject of this book, it is relevant to include the parallel contribution made by the second Vickers Wellington Shadow Factory, located at Squires Gate Airport near Blackpool. In December 1939, the Air Ministry had approved plans for a third Wellington Factory to be located there. As in the case of Chester, this plant was to be owned by the government and operated by Vickers-Armstrongs. However, unlike Chester, which handled assembly only, the Blackpool unit was set up (from Weybridge and not Chester) for complete aircraft manufacture from the detail stages. Much bigger than its near-neighbour, this factory had its own machine shops from the outset and its own family of subcontractors.

When various prospective sites in Lancashire were being assessed for the location of an airfield to support the re-established English Electric aircraft manufacturing facility at Strand Road, Preston, although the then Preston-Blackburn airport seemed suitable, another site to the west of Preston was also in contention. This was also being examined by Vickers-Armstrongs for a possible Wellington Shadow Factory. Consequently questions arose about the two firms sharing the Grange Farm Airfield,

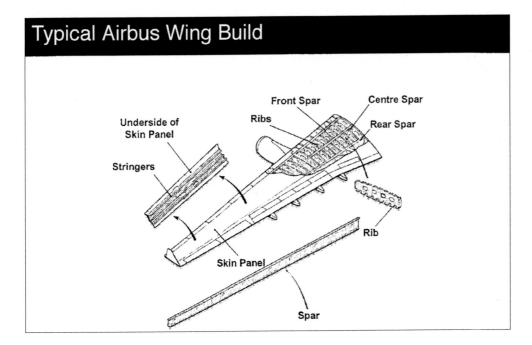

the relative timescales for completion, and whether or not the population of Preston could provide a big enough workforce for two large factories. In the end, the Grange Farm plan was abandoned (it was on low ground and a potential flood plain close to where the Warton Aerodrome was later built on rather higher ground). While English Electric opted for Samlesbury for its airfield facility, Vickers elected to establish its second northern Wellington Factory at Blackpool, a little further to the north-west, and which became operational from early 1940. The second assembly line was established at nearby Stanley Park (the original Blackpool municipal airport) in October 1941.

Although, like with Chester, a contract was also received for the production of 300 Vickers Warwick aircraft, and shortly afterwards cancelled, the entire aircraft output of the Blackpool unit during the Vickers-Armstrongs management period consisted of Wellingtons. The first Blackpool-built aircraft was completed in July 1940 and the last in October 1945; a total of 3,406 were made (430 of them at Stanley Park).

Similar to Chester, 11,250 prefabricated houses were built at Blackpool between September 1945 and April 1948, before the plant was put on a 'care and maintenance' basis until finally vacated by Vickers on 18 October 1949. It was later turned over to the Hawker Aircraft Company to resume aircraft production with the Hunter jet fighter from 1952. The former aircraft factory is now a substantial industrial estate, retaining most of the wartime buildings, and Stanley Park is now the home of the Blackpool Zoo.

# From Bomber to Bungalow – A Peace Dividend

During the Second World War, domestic house building came to a standstill in favour of the nationally vital industries, notably aircraft production, needed to support the war effort. But before the end of hostilities, as well as considering the anticipated post-war commercial aircraft requirements and specifications in association with the recommendations of the Brabazon Committees, the British Government also turned its attention to the major problem of housing. Those made homeless by the Blitz and the rehabilitation of those coming home from war service were both pressing concerns. There was a predicted major surplus of aircraft skills and materials in the immediate post-war years, until such time as the new civil and military aircraft designs could be

*The large-scale machining of Airbus wing skin panels. This process has consistently involved some of the largest machine tools anywhere in the world since the inauguration of the programme in 1971. Taking a lead from the pioneering work by Vickers-Weybridge in large-scale structural machining from the late 1950s, long-bed machines at Broughton have incorporated vacuum suction beds for securing the panels during the high-speed cutting operation, and beam-mounted, multiple vacuum suction pads for lifting and transporting the very large and flexible panels, and both of which methods have since been continuously deployed at Broughton with successive new developments of these specialised machines.*

put into production. To complement the Government's plans for a National Health Scheme mooted by the Beveridge Plan of 1944, the MAP commendably organised a competition between aircraft firms for the large-scale production of AIROH (Aircraft Industry Research On Housing) aluminium prefabricated houses which could be quickly and easily erected on prepared foundations.

The contest for these ingenious utilitarian constructions was won by the Bristol Aeroplane Company and the Vickers-Chester Factory joined forces with the Bristol-managed Shadow Factory at Weston-Super-Mare, Vickers at Blackpool and Blackburn at Dumbarton, Scotland. A production order for 11,250 units – 'Prefabs' as they were universally known – was placed at Chester, and a similar number at Blackpool.

This welcome interim work not only provided a most necessary contribution to the revitalisation of post-war Britain but also enabled Vickers to continue the employment of many Chester and Blackpool staff and workpeople in what in today's parlance would be called a 'Peace Dividend'.

# The de Havilland Dynasty

The impending completion of all manufacturing work at Chester under the Vickers management in April 1948 meant that the company was scheduled to close and vacate the factory completely soon afterwards with the loss of many jobs.

Fortuitously again, however, the de Havilland Aircraft Company (DH) at Hatfield, Hertfordshire, had an order book worth some £10 million – a considerable sum and business volume at that time. This was principally for its new post-war designs – the Brabazon-specified Dove twin-engined light civil and military transport and the later production Vampire twin-boom jet fighter (after the initial output had been handled by English Electric at Preston, Lancashire). The Board of Trade also considered that exports were vital to boost the depressed post-wart economy. These imaginative new DH types were proving widely suitable in helping to fulfill this national mandate in response to the rapid growth of post-war commercial avaiation, contrasting with the still uneasy peace that was generating a new round of rearmament by Commonwealth, Allied and friendly nations overseas.

Besides turning out a Dove every working day, the expanding production of the Vampire, plus the continuing output of the Mosquito and Hornet piston-engined fighters, the Hatfield plant was being prepared to take on the development of the new Comet jetliner. It had, however, insufficient space and resources to cope with this growth. As had already been realised at the time of the wartime construction of the second large DH Factory at Leavesden, noted earlier, for various natural considerations it was not practicable to extend the factory in the Hatfield area. It was therefore decided to lease, if possible, another large factory elsewhere to provide the considerable extra capacity that was urgently needed.

The decision in 1947 to embark upon a large expansion of the company's productive capacity had four main beneficial results. Firstly, the large contracts obtained from overseas purchasers, before Britain itself adopted a rearmament policy, enabled a strong manufacturing organisation to be built up, ready to expand further when the government did decide to rearm. Secondly, the overseas business speeded the development of the Vampire night fighter and trainer and the Venom variants. Thirdly, these exports consolidated the military readiness of several Commonwealth and other countries. Fourthly, they brought in millions of pounds' worth of nationally important export trade.

Fortuitously, the impending surplus Chester Factory was considered to be ideal. Consequently, in its 1948 Annual Report, de Havilland announced: 'For various national considerations, we are not able to expand our factories in Hertfordshire and the London area much beyond their present size, and to cope with the export business obtained, it has been necessary for us to secure a lease on a further factory near Chester. This is a modern factory, about as large as our main factory at Hatfield, and we expect to be able to develop an efficient aircraft assembly organisation there'. Moreover, the Chester Factory was better planned as it had not grown piecemeal, and was the most modern factory in Europe at that time. Hence, after Wilfred Nixon, DH managing director, and Harry Povey, production director, had gained a good first impression by flying over the Chester site in a Dove, the factory was allocated to de Havilland.

As a result, during February 1948, key DH personnel occupied an office in the factory assembly area and began planning the resumption of large-scale aircraft production. As Vickers-Armstrongs was finishing its prefab housing work at one end of the main assembly area, aircraft jigs from Hatfield were being installed at the other. After the formal hand-over ceremony on 1 July 1948, the management of the site was progressively taken over by DH during the rest of that year and the renewed aircraft production work moved ahead quickly.

The first of the many major DH aircraft programmes at Chester was the completion of the end phase of the wooden Mosquito and its wood-and-metal counterpart, the Hornet. The first of the ninety-six Chester-built Mosquitoes flew on 30 September 1948, only eight months after the first technicians had arrived from Hatfield, by which time the production preparation for the Hornet and the Vampire (with export orders for Sweden and Switzerland) was also well under way. The first of the 149 Hornets flew in March 1949, and Vampire deliveries had started before the end of that year. (The Vampire gave Chester its first experience of turbine power and was the first RAF fighter to exceed 500mph). By December 1949 the total personnel employed at DH Chester had reached 652 and a recruitment campaign was proving very successful.

The early 1950s saw much diversity of DH designs quantity-built at Chester. In 1950, when the Chipmunk basic pilot trainer aircraft, designed by the de Havilland Company of Canada, was adopted by the Royal Air Force, the bulk of the production in the UK was handed to Chester and 889 of these versatile aircraft were built there during the next seven years. Production of the Dove was transferred to Chester in 1951, to share the shop floor with the Vampire night fighter. The following year, they were joined by the Vampire Trainer and the Venom derivative of the Vampire.

The first of the 424 Chester-built Vampire Trainers and 834 Venoms were completed in 1952. Thus in only its first four years under DH management the Chester Factory had produced aircraft of eight distinct types – seven of which were being built simultaneously (Mosquito production having ceased in November 1950).

In 1953, DH employed 12 test pilots to cope with the large numbers of Vampires, Venoms, Chipmunks, Doves and Herons that were being produced to meet the dual requirements of the post-Korean war rearmament programme and the rapid growth of civil air transport.

The year 1953 saw the start of production batches of the Dove's larger four-engined derivative, the Heron, with 244 and 140, respectively, being built at Chester when production of both types was completed in 1967. Significantly, the Heron output included a fleet of four VIP aircraft built for HM The Queen's Flight.

The Comet jetliner, first flown at Hatfield on 27 July 1949, showed early market promise on both sides of the Atlantic. This success led to de Havilland and Short Brothers and Harland establishing an agreement whereby a second Comet production line would be set up at Belfast in Northern Ireland. On 31 October 1952, DH announced that some component manufacture for the Comet had already started at Chester and that it intended to lay down a third Comet line there. All three lines would make the Comet 2 and were expected to make the changeover to the Comet 3 in 1956-1957. The long-term plan was based on Hatfield being the development and pre-production base, with quantity production shared between the three factories (in similar fashion to the wartime Shadow Factory concept).

Work on the Comet began at Chester, initially sharing with Hatfield the production of the Comet 2 for British Overseas Airways Corporation (BOAC), and notably including extensive use of the metal-bonding process. However, when the first of the twenty-five Comet 2s in the initial production plan was nearing completion in 1954, disaster struck the programme. There had been three tragic aircraft losses in mysterious circumstances in BOAC service and production of the first twelve machines in progress there had to be abruptly suspended. Components that had been completed at the similarly moribund Belfast line were later also shipped to Chester. Restarting production in 1955 by reworking the Mk.2 airframes with strengthened fuselages, principally to serve as transports with the Royal Air Force, meant that the first (and only) Comet 2 to be completed and flown at Chester was XK716. It was made for the RAF and was delivered to No.216 Squadron on 7 May 1957 and named 'Cephus'. Chester's Comet 2 up-date programme was completed in 1957. The following year, when the full cause of the accidents had been ascertained by the Royal Aircraft Establishment (RAE) at Farnborough, and the remedy devised, a Comet 4 production line was established at Chester to augment the Hatfield line. The first of this much modified and extended version from the Chester line, G-APDE, was delivered to BOAC in 1959 and production of the Comet 4 continued there until 1964. Overall, Chester had built forty-two complete Comet airframes of the total Hatfield/Chester output of 117 units (including test examples).

Achieving the huge production build-up and export performance at Chester, handling the main flow of DH civil and military transport and combat aircraft during the 1950s and 1960s, was not without very real difficulties, especially in the recruitment of suitable labour in the largely agrarian locality. This required extensive training. So, early in 1949, a branch of the famed de Havilland Technical School (originally formed at Hatfield in 1928) was opened to support the prolific apprenticeship scheme, and another for tradesman, within the factory. Workers were attracted from as far afield as Belfast and Glasgow. Long-distance bus services were operated for daily commuters from centres as far distant as Liverpool, Warrington and Crewe. The local authorities at Chester, Hawarden and Mold also greatly assisted with new housing.

Tooling and equipping was a constant priority, especially with the introduction of the much larger-scale and vastly more complicated Comet jetliner, with its much higher man-hour content and new production processes.

# Under the Hawker Siddeley Banner

When the British Government enforced the consolidation of the UK aircraft industry in 1960 into two main airfarme groups – British Aircraft Corporation (BAC) and the Hawker Siddeley Group (HSG), which had originally been formed in 1935 – the hitherto independent de Havilland Aircraft Company was taken into the latter group. This was the second of the many parental organisational changes to embrace the Chester unit. It was, however, a seamless process at the working level and the pioneering DH name continued in its new designation as part of the Hawker Siddeley de Havilland Division in conjunction with Hatfield.

Assembly of the DH Canada Beaver light transport aircraft, chosen by the British Army Air Corps, began at Chester in 1961, continuing into 1962 and resuming with a repeat order in 1967;

*The completely modernised, extended and equipped and highly productive BAe Systems Airbus UK Broughton Factory in 2000 (August).*

a total of forty-six aircraft were eventually built. Production of the de Havilland Christchurch-designed Sea Vixen twin-engined naval all-weather fighter began in 1962 and continued until 1966 with the completion of thirty aircraft for the Royal Navy.

On 13 August 1962, the first flight took place at Hatfield of the distinctive DH125 corporate business jet that was soon to become a veritable lifesaver for Chester. Intended as a jet-powered successor to the Dove, the concept of the diminutive transport aircraft had been first revealed publicly in 1961 as the: 'World's first jet aircraft specifically designed as a corporate communications aircraft' and 'a jet airliner in miniature'. Because Hatfield was becoming heavily involved with the development of the much bigger Trident airliner, Chester thus became the exclusive production source for the 125 and the first batch was laid down there at the beginning of 1962.

The Hawker Siddeley Group of engineering and aviation companies was restructured on 1 July 1963, and its aviation interests incorporated in a new subsidiary, Hawker Siddeley Aviation (HSA). Accordingly, Chester was brought within the HSA de Havilland Division, and all but the longest-established DH products were re-designated with the 'HS' prefix.

But with the end of the Comet line in sight, rumours were rife that both the Chester Factory and the Hawarden Airfield might have to close. However, it was the encouraging build-up of orders for the 125 that doubtless saved the day and kept a large part of the factory busy through the 1960s.

It was then that the long-famous de Havilland company name disappeared completely, passing into history on 1 April 1965 after 17 years currency at the Chester plant (and 45 years altogether since established by its pioneer signatory, Sir Geoffrey de Havilland, on 25 September 1920). HSA abandoned all of the original company names of its constituent divisions in favour of geographical designations. Paradoxically, however, the bonus was that the Chester name came forward formally again when it was embodied in the title of the new entity, the HSA Hatfield-Chester Division.

Between 1965 and 1967, two Chester-built speculative Comet 4Cs were re-allocated to become development prototypes for the Nimrod, the worlds' first pure-jet maritime reconnaissance and anti-submarine patrol aircraft, to replace the Avro Shackleton of RAF Coastal Command (a large batch of which had earlier been overhauled and up-graded at Chester). An assembly line was started in 1966 with the production of the main fuselage and other components. These were then

21

*The new Airbus UK Broughton 'West Factory' seen looking across the main Hawarden Airfield runway towards the original 'East Factory'. Purpose-designed as the wing manufacturing centre for the new giant generation A380 'Super Jumbo' airliner, the new £350 million plant was built and equipped in record time, beginning in August 2002, ceremoniously opened in July 2002 and the first wing structure was dispatched for final assembly in Toulouse, in south-west France, on 5 April 2004.*

transported to the HSA Manchester Division Factory at Woodford for completion with the lower fuselage, final assembly and delivery. The Chester involvement in this programme ceased in 1970 after forty-one airframe sets had been built there.

In a significant step for HSA, following a number of exchanges for new airliner design concepts with other major European aircraft manufacturers in the mid-1960s, the company became the UK industrial partner when a tripartite Memorandum of Understanding (MOU) was signed by the British, French and German governments. It was signed on 26 September 1967, and set out the plans for the design of a new-generation wide-body, twin-aisle, twin-jet airliner. The agreement was to provide the expertise required for the advanced aerodynamic design and manufacture of the wing which HS had acquired with its Trident programme and for which there was no equivalent within the two continental partner industries. HS kept faith in the programme, even after the British Government withdrew its support in March 1969. When the Airbus Industrie (AI) airliner programme was launched on 29 May 1969 by the French and German governments, HSA continued to participate in a private sub-contract role, taking responsibility for the design and manufacture of the complete main wing structure for the definitive Airbus 250-seat A300B. HSA then sustained its involvement in the programme when AI was formally constituted in December 1970.

Significantly, this action resulted in a new and enduring dimension of scale, capability and output for Chester from 1971 with the start of the construction work for this major new multinational civil aircraft venture. In turn, it lead to the installation of some of the largest and most advanced structural machine tools and manufacturing jigs anywhere in the world.

The first completed A300B wing set was dispatched on 23 November 1971. The transportation of the huge structures was initially by road on custom-designed trailers to either Manchester or Liverpool airports, where they were loaded into a 'Super Guppy' specialist adaptation of the original Boeing Stratocruiser military tanker/civil transport aircraft devised for carrying such outsize loads. They were then delivered to the VFW plant at Bremen in Germany for equipping, prior to being flown on to the AI final assembly centre at Aerospatiale at Toulouse in Southern France. This process thus ensured that no structural component would ever be out of production working for more than 48 hours.

# British Aerospace and Airbus Wings the World Over

Six years on from the start of the Airbus venture at Chester, the plant was again re-designated as a result of the nationalisation edict of the British aircraft industry by the then Labour Government. In the process, the Hawker Siddeley Group's aviation and guided weapons interests ceded into the newly established British Aerospace (BAe). After 'vesting day' for the new company on 29 April 1977, the formal constitution came into being on 1 January 1978. The former Hawker Siddeley Aviation (HSA) company became, in turn, a member of the Aircraft Group with the Chester unit and name continuing within the BAe Hatfield-Chester Division. Agreement at the industrial level between the AI consortium partners was initialed on 18 August 1978 and ratified by the respective governments on 27 October so that BAe joined AI on 1 January 1979 as a full decision-making partner with a 20 per cent shareholding. As well as the expanding Airbus airliner customer base, sales of the (now further re-designated) BAe 125 were likewise continuing steadily and the sale of the 500th aircraft was announced in October 1980, after a record-breaking sales year in 1979 during which fifty-five aircraft were sold. The 100th set of Airbus wings was also delivered from Chester to Bremen in June 1979.

Further corporate organisational change came on 1 January 1981 with the formation of British Aerospace PLC, following its flotation on the Stock Market and substantial re-privatisation (with the return to full privatisation completed on 10 May 1985). It was also in 1981 that BAe purchased the freehold of the hitherto leased Chester Factory site and Hawarden Airfield from the Ministry of Defence. The first wing set for the A310, the second member of the AI family, left the assembly jigs at Chester on 7 April 1981 and after equipping at Filton was dispatched to Bremen for completion on 17 May 1981.

*The new autonomous 52,300 sqm site area Broughton 'North Factory' – physically larger than the new London Wembley Stadium and employing more than 650 people – for assembley of the carbon-fibre wing box structures for the new-generation Airbus A350XWB (eXtra Wide Body) airliner, ceremoniously opened by Prime Minister, David Cameron, and Welsh First Minister, Carwyn Jones, on 13 October 2011, and delivering two wing sets a month in 2014 and rising to ten sets a month by 2018*

Yet another change came in early 1989, following the formation of British Aerospace (Commercial Aircraft) Ltd on 1 January and the establishment of three autonomous business divisions of that company a month later; the Chester site became part of the new BAe Airbus Ltd – in conjunction with the BAe Filton (Bristol) site. However, this change also meant the loss of the Chester headline name after 24 years of use – seven years longer than the site had operated under the de Havilland name banner.

Airbus wing production built up at an almost exponential rate through the 1980s. The first wing set for the new single-aisle addition to the AI family, the 'reference standard' A320 medium-haul twin-jet, was despatched from Chester to BAe Filton on 28 November 1985, to a new A320 Wing Equipping Centre. Delivery was initially by road and sea via Plymouth, and later by Super Guppy aircraft, to Toulouse for final assembly. This sequence continued until July 1993 with the completion of the 453rd A320 wing set, whence the equipping of these wings was reverted to Chester.

The highlights of 1989 were the commissioning on 1 August of the new £5 million 'link' building (between the original main assembly area and the former flight shed) and delivery of the 600th Airbus wing set in September. The first wing set for the A340 wide-body, twin-aisle, four-jet, long-range jetliner was delivered in August 1990, the 250th A320 wing set (from Filton) in July 1991, and the first wing set for the twin-engine wide-body A330 counterpart of the A340 in September. This coincided with the opening of a new £3.2 million Airbus Wing Despatch Centre.

During the 1990s, the aging Super Guppy aircraft were replaced by a fleet of five Super Transporter 'Beluga' aircraft adapted from its own A300-600 and incorporating Chester-made wings. Following improvements to the main Hawarden runway in 1996, these extraordinary aircraft have since transported all Airbus wings (except those for the outsize A380) direct instead of from Manchester airport after road transfer. Those for the A300/A310/A330/A340/A350XWB wide-body lineage are first flown to Bremen for the equipping before proceeding to Toulouse for final assembly. Those for the A318/A319/A320/A321 twin-jet family are flown, pre-equipped, direct to Toulouse (A320) and to Hamburg (A318, A319 and A321) for final assembly in the complete aircraft.

The 2,000th Airbus wing set was delivered in February 1999, the year in which Airbus Industrie commendably first won an equal market share of the intensely competitive global market for mainstream jetliners against its formidable American competitor, the long-established Boeing Company, and to the considerable benefit to the Chester Factory. Appropriately, British Aerospace Airbus also won a Queen's Award for Export Achievement that year 'in recognition of the significant contribution that the export of Airbus wings makes to the UK economy'.

# Raytheon and Hawker Beechcraft Corporate Jets

Coincident with the corporate organisational change in 1989, resulting in the formation of British Aerospace (Commercial Aircraft) Ltd noted earlier, Chester also became the output centre of BAe Corporate Jets Ltd, the new autonomous company responsible for the continuing BAe 125 business. Renamed Corporate Jets Ltd in May 1992, on 1 June 1993 this company was sold to the Raytheon Aircraft Company (RAC) of the USA – which has continued to apply the original 'Hawker' prefix to its latest derivative models. Airframe component kits continue to be made by Airbus UK at Broughton under a subcontract agreement before being shipped for final assembly by RAC in the USA. RAC itself also became established in its own right at Broughton, initially as Raytheon Aircraft Systems Ltd (later Hawker Beechcraft) and later also as Raytheon Systems Ltd, handling the ASTOR (Airborne Stand-Off Radar) programme for the UK Ministry of Defence. The twin hangar complex was acquired by Marshall Aviation Services in August 2013.

# BAE Systems and Airbus UK into the New Millennium

The Filton (Bristol) and Broughton teaming began operating from 31 March 2000 as Airbus UK Ltd, a wholly owned subsidiary of BAE Systems – which itself had become effective from

30 November 1999 with the merger integration of the former British Aerospace (BAe) and GEC-Marconi Electronic Systems (MES) companies – and became operationally effective from 1 January 2001. This was in anticipation of the transformation of the now anachronistic French Groupment d'Interet Economique (GIE), legal format of the four-nation Airbus Industrie organisation (UK, France, Germany and Spain), into a fully commercially accountable Single Corporate Entity (SCE). The new concept Airbus Integrated Company (AIC) was announced on 23 June 2000 and was formally constituted simply as 'Airbus' (instead of the previous Airbus Industrie) on 15 June 2001. It was in the same form of a French S.A.S. (Societe par Actions Simplifiee) or simplified stock company, in which Airbus UK represented the BAE Systems 20 per cent shareholding. The newly constituted European Aeronautic Defence and Space Company (EADS) – which was formed on 10 July 2000 by the merger of the French Aerospatiale-Matra, German DaimlerChrysler Aerospace and Spanish CASA – now had the remaining 80 per cent shareholding in the new Airbus company. In this simplified and unified organisational arrangement of Airbus interests, Airbus UK became part of the 'stand-alone' Airbus company when it became fully operational in January 2001 and the Broughton wing manufacturing facility continued to operate integrally with the Airbus UK management, design and manufacturing centre at Filton (Bristol). In addition to being the wing 'Centre of Excellence', the company also has responsibility for the design and supply for fuel systems and, for some Airbus variants, integration of the landing gear – plus the continuing supply of wings and fuselages for Hawker jets.

At that point, the 450-acre Broughton Factory/Hawarden Aerodrome site employed a workforce of around 4,300 people from north-east Wales, Chester, the Wirral and Liverpool (more than three-quarters of its peak wartime personnel complement). It was injecting £3.5 million a week in wages, goods and services into the economy within a thirty-mile radius of the plant.

Major capital investment in new factory equipping and extensions was implemented during 1999 for the production of the wings for the four-engined 335-450 seat A340-500 and -600 extended-range developments. The first sets of wings (with 100ft long skin panels) for these two important new committed derivatives, was delivered in April 2000. Those for the 107-seat single-aisle A318, the smallest in the entire Airbus range, were completed in August 2001. The significant milestone of the delivery of the 3000th Airbus wing set (i.e. 6,000 individual wing structures) was reached on 18 February 2002.

Known as the A3XX during its conceptual years, the official launch on 19 December 2000 of the industrial programme for the completely new giant-generation 480 to 650-seat double-deck Airbus A380 commercial airliner – the world's largest and signaling a new era in world civil aviation – was the next major challenge for the newly reconstituted Airbus enterprise and particularly for Airbus UK. Consequently, a considerable increase in employment, work throughput and export earnings was portended for the Broughton site. A £530 million repayable UK Government loan investment committed in May 2000 to the launch of the A380 was complemented by BAE Systems' own planned investment of £230 million in the site over the next five years. The Welsh National Assembly First Secretary also announced on 24 September 2000 a Welsh Development Agency financial package grant totaling £19.5 million to support training and skills development to also enable continuing capital and skills investment at Broughton for the manufacture of Airbus wings and Raytheon corporate jets. Significantly, these grants also confirmed that the manufacture of the A380 wing structure had been secured for the North Wales site, thereby preserving the 3,000 existing jobs and creating a minimum of 1,700 new ones.

# New Giant Generation – New Factory

The maturity of the A380 manufacturing programme has since resulted in a wholly new purpose-built wing manufacturing plant and other supporting developments at Broughton, which were required to be built in record time. The massive £350 million and 900,000 sq.ft. construction – the largest and most advanced free-standing industrial building in the UK – was built by Dartford, Kent-based Laing O'Rourke, Britain's largest privately owned construction company, builders of the second Severn Bridge, the almost identically sized Terminal 5 main building at London-Heathrow airport and the new London St Pancras International rail terminal, and is the leading management contractor for the London 2012 Olympics. Built on an entirely 'greenfield' site, it was completed from initial ground-breaking in August 2001 to full operation and the delivery of the first A380 wing set in April 2004. As well as the installation of the corresponding new-generation equipment and tooling, the new factory also incorporates an environmentally innovative and highly efficient Combined Heat and Power System (CHP). Known as the Broughton 'West Factory', the new plant is located conveniently close to the River Dee to facilitate the short road transfer of the completed outsize wing structures to the first stage of their delivery by sea. The original plant is now known as the 'East Factory' (because of the respective geographical locations of the now two discrete plants on the overall Broughton site and separated by the Hawarden Airfield runway). Another £75 million has also been invested site-wide in new manufacturing equipment installations for the A380, the civil engineering contractor for the building extensions in the East Factory being AMEC, the world's' third largest civil engineering and project management group.

## Building the World's Largest Airliner Wings

The sheer size and weight of the high-performance A380 wings not only required a new purpose-built factory construction but also the harnessing of the latest manufacturing techniques and equipment to achieve the requisite technical performance. The key new enabling manufacturing facilities notably include the latest long-bed wing skin panel and stringer machine tools; third-generation automated low-voltage electromagnetic riveter (LVER) machines; and the, hitherto only laboratory-scale, automated creep forming (ACF) autoclave technology.

## Transport Logistics

The exceptional size and weight of the A380 equipped wing box structures also meant that they where too large to be transported by the aerial means that Airbus had been using up to this point – first with the 'Super Guppy' aircraft, and since 1966 superceded by the Airbus A300-600ST Super Transporter 'Beluga' with the world's most voluminous aircraft cargo hold. Consequently, Airbus has devised a uniquely innovative logistics system with the introduction of a multi-modal transport system (MMTS) deploying custom-built vehicles that operate an integrated transport supply network of road, river and sea routes linking all the major European A380 major airframe component manufacturing centres with the final assembly centre at Toulouse.

## Airbus UK and Broughton Today and Tomorrow

Major recent events have combined to set the pattern and the tempo of the Airbus UK and Broughton operation henceforth.

On 2 May 2006, BAE Systems announced its decision to relinquish its 20 per cent shareholding in Airbus and completed the sale to the Franco-German-Spanish European Aeronautic Defence and Space (EADS) company for 2.75 billion Euros on 13 October 2006 – resulting in Airbus becoming a wholly-owned subsidiary of EADS and now comprising 80 per cent of its total business portfolio.

Following the signing of a Memorandum of Understanding (MOU) by Airbus and the National Development and Reform Commission of China (NRDC) on 4 December 2005, on 8 June 2006, it was announced that the site for an Airbus A319/A320 final assembly line in China would be at Tianjin Binhai New Coastal District, near Beijing. Ratified on 26 October 2006, with a framework agreement with a tripartite Chinese consortium comprising the Tianjin Free Trade Zone (TJFTZ) and the twin state-owned China Aviation Industry Corporations, AVIC I and II, Airbus owns 51 per cent and the Chinese members hold the remaining 49 per cent, subdivided as: TJFTZ 60 per cent, and AVIC I and II 20 per cent each. Chinese State Council approval came in mid-May 2007 and contract sealing on 28 June 2007. Significantly, Broughton engineers are playing a key role in this major new joint venture and the first A319 wing box built by AVIC I's Xi'an Aircraft Company (XAC) was accepted on 24 July 2007 and arrived at Broughton for equipping on 25 September 2007 (which is to be the next phase in China). Complete aircraft assembly will begin in August 2008 with first delivery in the first half of 2009, building up to four aircraft a month by 2011.

On 12 December 2006, technical and airworthiness integrity of the A380, powered by Rolls-Royce Trent 900 engines, was fully validated by simultaneous award of Joint European Aviation Safety Agency (EASA) and American Federal Aviation Administration (FAA) Type Certification, axiomatically confirming the integrity of the Broughton A380 wing manufacturing operation.

On 1 December 2006 EADS announced the industrial launch of the fully-remodeled 200 to 375-seat Airbus A350XWB (Extra Wide Body) family with a first flight scheduled for 2011 and first service delivery in 2013. With more than 60 per cent content of carbon-fibre primary structure, this will take Broughton into a whole new era of wing construction. Airbus has since announced a £400million (570 million Euros) investment in a two-to-three year plan beginning in 2008 to upgrade composite manufacturing capability at Broughton. A further £34 million is being invested in the development of 'greener' technology in a three-year Integrated Wing Aerospace Technology Validation Programme to maintain Airbus at the forefront of wing manufacture. Airbus and others are funding half, with the other £17 million from the Department of Business and Regulatory Reform and regional sources, including £1 million from the Welsh Assembly, towards the development of robotic equipment for wing box assembly.

Meanwhile, major production 'ramp-ups' are being implemented in 2014: the A320 family from the current 42 wing sets a month – plus support of the Chinese assembly line; A330 to 11 per month; and the A380XWB to two per month – with the total all-types Airbus order book standing at more than 14,000 aircraft. Hawker corporate jet production ceased in 2012 after 50 years of continuous production at Broughton.

Most significantly, on 28 February 2007 came the announcement of the ambitious Airbus-wide Power8 organizational restructuring plan, the core objective being: 'to make Airbus more efficient and competitive, so as to produce the most advanced and profitable products, and to serve its customers better in the future'. The new 'extended enterprise' business model constitutes a coalescing of manufacturing operations around four truly transnational core 'centres of excellence' organized around complete aircraft elements – together with the consolidation of a robust supply chain of large industrial partnerships to hasten the advance into the era of composite technology, notably including the Airbus UK Filton site. The Wing and Pylon Centre of Excellence embraced Broughton and Filton in the UK, the wing equipping part of Bremen in Germany, and St. Eloi, Toulouse, (engine pylons) in France. Aircraft final assembly lines are also to be streamlined with the wide-body A330/A350XWB/A380 family and the single-aisle A320 in Toulouse, and the full A318/A319/A320/A321 family in Hamburg, Germany.

In fulfilling this new mandate, the exceptional 75-year Broughton heritage, experience, skills, reputation and record bequeath a correspondingly enhanced capability and value. Now acknowledged as the most productive of the 10 Airbus manufacturing sites across Europe, the rampant Airbus market success portends yet greater business volume for the 6,500-strong Broughton workforce to maintain this outstandingly-accomplished facility at the forefront of the global aerospace industry for as far ahead as can currently be foreseen.

Airbus Broughton became an autonomous manufacturing plant in an Airbus-wide reorganization on 1 January 2013 and became part of the newly rebranded Airbus Group (superseding the former EADS company) on 1 January 2014.

*The new-generation Airbus A350XWB (eXtra Wide Body) twin-engined airliner and the newest challenge for Airbus and Broughton. Conceived as: 'A 200-375 seat airliner family to achieve a leap ahead of the Boeing 787 and a generation beyond the Boeing 777 with unequalled levels of fuel and economic efficiency with low environmental impact', it heralds an exciting new chapter in the ever-advancing Broughton story. The new highly swept and highly tapered wings will allow cruising speeds of up to Mach 0.89, incorporate innovative wing tips and high-lift systems, a new landing gear integration, new concept engine pylons, and the main wing torsion box structure includes a large proportion of carbon-fibre reinforced plastic (CFRP) – so taking Broughton into the era of composite technology on a correspondingly major scale.*

*Left: Sir Robert McLean, Chairman of Vickers (Aviation) Ltd, who approached the British Government in 1936 with the need for another Wellington Production Factory to augment the output at the Vickers parent plant at Weybridge. Centre: Trevor Westbrook, Vickers General Manager – Weybridge, Chester and Blackpool, who had transferred to Weybridge from Vickers-Supermarine at Southampton at the end of 1936 after having been the driving force in getting the all-metal Spitfire fighter into quantity production. Right: John Corby, de Havilland's first General Manager, Chester: 1949-58.*

*'Wellington Warriors': The Vickers-Chester management with a group of visiting Royal Air Force Wellingtom aircrew in 1940. Centre row, third from left: Ronnie Yapp, Commercial Manager (later Managing Director of Vickers Ltd). Fifth from left: Gordon Montgomery, Works Manager. Front row, first left: Maurice Hare, Chief Test Pilot. Centre: Bernard Duncan, Superintendent.*

# Management Personalities

After the initial short period at Chester, during which Gordon Montgomery was seconded from Weybridge as Assembly Manager (responsible for the first Chester-built Wellington), the General Manager of the Vickers-Armstrongs Weybridge, Chester and Blackpool units was the redoubtable Trevor Westbrook. He left the company on 30 March 1940 to join the Ministry of Aircraft Production (MAP), Lord Beaverbrook's wartime team of aircraft production expeditors. Under Westbrook, the Works Manager at the Chester Factory was E.R. 'Rex' Talamo (brought in from elsewhere in the Vickers Group), who went on to become the Superintendent after Westbrook vacated his office. Talamo was then replaced as Works Manager by Gordon Montgomery, who sadly died in 1941. Talamo was later transferred to the Vickers Spitfire Shadow Factory at Castle Bromwich, Birmingham, and was succeeded at Chester on 1 May 1940 by Bernard Duncan (who had previously been Experimental Manager at Weybridge and was succeeded there by the subsequently knighted George Edwards). Duncan then retained the office of Superintendent until 30 June 1948 when all Vickers activities ceased at the Chester Factory.

The de Havilland era at Chester was inaugurated by a small team from Hatfield, with Clem Pike, personal representative of Wilfred Nixon (DH Managing Director), in charge of preliminary arrangements. The first permanent appointments were: John Corby, General Manager; James Mackenzie, Production Manager; Sydney Statham, Factory Manager; Arthur Turner, Production Engineer; and David Brown, Chief Inspector. Successive 'directors-in-charge' during the subsequent de Havilland, Hawker Siddeley, British Aerospace, BAE Systems and now Airbus UK tenures (albeit with varying titles) were/are:

29

Arthur Turner, Production
Divisional Manager: 1959-
1961 (member of the original
team which re-opened Chester
for DH in 1948).

Jack Garston, Production
Manager: 1961; Works
Manager: 1962-69; Executive
Director and Works Manager:
1970-71; Executive Director and
General Manager: 1972-77.
(Works Manager at wartime
Cranage satellite.)

Percy Edwards, Director and
General Manager: 1977-79.

Arthur Rowland, Director
and General Manager:
1980-84.

John Gillbanks, Divisional
Director and General
Manager: 1984-88.

Shaun Dyke, Director and
General Manager: 1989-
1995.

David Waring, Director of
Manufacturing and Product
Executive Hawker Jet: 1995-
97.

Bill Travis, Director of
Manufacturing: 1997-99.

Brian Fleet, Director,
Manufacturing, Airbus UK:
1999-2001; Senior V.P., Head
of Centre for Excellence, Wing,
Airbus UK: 2004–2011.

Garston, Gillbanks and Dyke also served as presidents of the Chester Branch of the Royal
Aueronautical Society.

# One

# Building a Bomber
# Birthplace

Construction of a large-scale aircraft factory and supporting airfield on a 'green-field' site is rare. The massive construction task for the Chester Shadow Factory was compounded by urgency, and the fact that the site was poorly drained and had a significant sloping aspect requiring major levelling.

The civil engineering contract for the factory was awarded to Sir William Arrol and Son of Clydeside. Ground-breaking began on 14 December 1938 and the entire complex was completed in nine months, long before the advent of modern-day earth-moving equipment and tower cranes. It was fully operational by the outbreak of the Second World War in September 1939. The factory was the largest covered building in Europe with a total floor area of 1.5 million sq.ft. Large elements of the fabric of the original construction are still in use today.

*The virgin construction site, indicating the rural nature of the area and the preparation necessary prior to construction. The orientation is shown by the L-shaped spur from (what is today) the A5104 Chester Road (lower centre) which became the main entrance to the complex, leading to the main office block.*

The construction site had initially appeared level, but there was actually a fall of about 7ft from south-west to north-east. This necessitated the excavation of 4ft at the former end and the filling up of 3ft at the latter end. Trenches had to be cut for the new drainage system to direct existing gullies away from the factory site. Despite excessive winter flooding, small temporary offices for Arrols and Vickers-Armstrongs were erected and the first strip of top soil removed before Christmas 1938. The railway spur line sidings, adjoining the London, Midland & Scottish (LMS) line (now no longer in existence) also were delivering the first drainage pipes. However, by January 1939 the exceptional winter rainfall meant that the site became a sea of mud and a network of jubilee tracks had to be laid (centre) to enable the completion of the earth-moving operation.

By early March 1939, the first vertical steelwork was being erected. By the end of the month, the steel erection was well advanced and a start had been made with the concrete columns for the offices. A temporary rail track (foreground) encircled the building work to enable materials to be transported direct to the point of use. Poles carrying temporary lighting for night work were erected around the whole site.

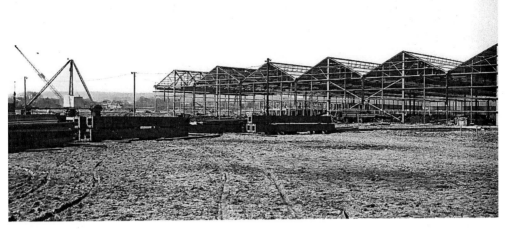

Steel erection of the 'low' part of the main factory building nearing completion, pending attachment of the side-wall panels.

Steel erection of the 'high' main assembly area and 'Northern Light' roof structure. The large trestles under the transverse roof support beams were temporary construction aids prior to this area becoming a completely clear and uninterrupted roof span. The whole factory was later traversed by a unique and powerful overhead crane system attached to these beams, which could lift up to ten tons at any one point using two five-ton cranes. Complete wings and power-plants could be swiftly lifted into position from their assembly feed-in areas alongside the main wheeled-trolley Wellington fuselage line. Twenty years later, this same crane system would enable Comet jetliner wings and fuselages to be united in minutes and the mating operation to be completed in seven hours rather than the seven days taken in the size-constrained de Havilland parent factory at Hatfield.

The main office block and forecourt, fronting the first bay of the main factory construction, was finished and occupied in mid-September 1939 (prior to the later addition of a second floor and hipped roof). It has the Vickers-Armstrongs Ltd signage prominently displayed above, and on, the entrance reception doorway. Many of the original Vickers-Armstrongs 'V-A'-identified lamp standards (bottom right), that were to line the site approach road, survived until recently when they had to be removed because of 'concrete fatigue'.

Although the Chester Factory location was believed remote from possible enemy air attack, camouflage was applied early to the front of the main office block. This was made from the hessian used for protecting the setting concrete during the wet winter weather.

*The main factory, largely completed externally, and camouflage-painted in mid-November 1939. The adjoining land was still very muddy and relying on horse-drawn transport in many areas.*

*The north-west corner of the engine-running and flight shed near completion in mid-November 1939. Sliding doors are being fitted, as is a section of the fencing (bottom left), which ultimately enclosed the whole factory site.*

35

By mid-November 1939, the brickwork and roofing of the 1,500-seat staff canteen was well advanced, with the works transport vehicle park being accommodated underneath.

The interior of the staff canteen main hall with self-service on either side. The entertainment stage facility at the far end was frequently featured in the famous national morale-boosting BBC lunchtime radio programme, Workers Playtime, announcing, as wartime security demanded, that is was 'coming to you from an aircraft factory somewhere in the North of England.'

# The Hawarden Aerodrome

The pre-existence of flying activity on the original Hawarden Estate was not only a significant factor in the Air Ministry requisitioning the site for the flight test and delivery of the output of the adjoining Shadow Factory but also meant that it naturally lent the Hawarden name to the whole operation in the minds of many. It was located on fertile but poorly drained agricultural land reclaimed from the River Dee when a five-mile section between Shotton and Chester was canalised in the eighteenth century. A 100-acre stretch of this area had been used from 1935-1937 as a relief landing ground (RLG) for RAF Sealand, three miles to the north-west.

During construction of the factory from mid-December 1938, the land was compulsorily purchased and it comprised of about a third of the area of the present site, on a strip of land lying south to north. The civil engineering contractor was Bernard Sunley and Co. Ltd. Despite considerable land in-filling and the installation of sophisticated pipe-work, the absence of natural drainage had serious consequences over successive winters, not only hampering construction of the factory but also wartime operation of the airfield. Most of the grubbing of trees and hedgerows was only made possible by using pairs of steam ploughing traction engines located 100 yards apart and hauling large drag buckets and multi-share ploughs between them on heavy wire ropes.

Enlarged during 1939, and taking advantage of the high local unemployment, Hawarden Rural District Council co-operated in building new housing estates for the airfield and factory workers, the first at Broad Oak, Broughton, with others following at East Saltney and Ewloe. After the first hangars had been erected in early 1940, the airfield suffered its first and only air raid on the night of 14 November 1940, the night of the infamous air attack on Coventry, damaging twenty-eight aircraft in two hangars.

Although never used for operational flying, the main wartime occupation of the airfield was by the major RAF Maintenance Unit (No.48 MU) formed on 6 March 1940 (ultimately disbanded on 1 July 1957). The unit also occupied most of the surrounding fields with aircraft storage and all the hangars (most of which still survive). No.7 Operational Training Unit was also formed there on 15 June 1940 (becoming No.57 OTU) for fighter and fighter-reconnaissance pilots and Air Transport Auxiliary (ATA) Ferry Pilots Pools (FPP) for the delivery of new aircraft, occupying hangars near the control tower. Fighter training was perfected using a early form of flight simulator, locally devised, known as the 'Hawarden Trainer' and the Hawarden OTU became one of the most important in the country for final Spitfire training.

The RAF's main function at Hawarden during the immediate post-war years was the scrapping of many hundreds of surplus wartime aircraft, although it did continue to prepare new ones for service use on a much reduced scale. When de Havilland took over the factory in 1948, the airfield was initially used for flight-testing by arrangement with the Air Ministry – three jointly sponsored Battle of Britain displays were also held there in September 1951, 1954 and 1956. Continuing in dual use by the RAF and DH, the military station accommodated No.173 Squadron to ferry aircraft in the UK, until its disbandment on 2 September 1957. RAF Hawarden station was ultimately closed on 31 March 1959, due to major cuts in defence expenditure, after which de Havilland took over the complete site, inheriting the vacated hangars and buildings, thereby ending Hawarden's twenty-year association with the RAF (although a gliding school survived until 1963).

In 1960, DH attempted to generate revenue by starting commercial services, at what was officially known as 'Hawarden Airport', which continued spasmodically until June 1979. Much further development of the aerodrome has taken place over the last 20 years – most notably, the strengthening and widening of the ends of the main 6,000ft/2,043m runway and the provision of 'bat-handle' ground-turning areas for the specialised wing transport aircraft in 1996. This has enabled all Airbus wing structures (except those of the new A380) to be despatched direct from Hawarden, instead of either Manchester or Liverpool airports.

*Overhead the Broughton Factory/Hawarden Aerodrome complex in July 1947, two years after the end of the exhausting Second World War, transformed to build prefabricated houses as a 'peace dividend', with many war-surplus aircraft still parked awaiting disposal. The remarkable wartime production record by Vickers-Armstrongs of 5,786 large bomber aircraft (and the repair of many more) was clear testimony not only to the intelligent design, construction and operation of the complex as an autonomous aircraft manufacturing plant, but also to the success of the British Government's imaginative 'Shadow Factory Scheme.'*

*The geographical orientation of the factory and main 05-23 runway running parallel to it, is approximately south-west to north-east from the main entrance end of the site (the orientation of this photograph being from South (top) to North (bottom) along the axis of the secondary runway). The linking railway spur from the LMS, noted earlier, can be seen running across the top left corner alongside the main factory complex.*
(Central Registry of Air Photography for Wales)

## *Two*

# The Vickers Bastion of Big Bomber Production

The designation of the Chester Shadow Factory for large-scale production of the Vickers Wellington from scratch, with a largely untrained workforce, remote from the main Vickers plant at Weybridge, posed a major challenge in addition to having to cope with the complex geodetic ('basketweave') airframe structure. Essentially operating as a 'parent works', the manufacture of all components was subcontracted, including nearby dispersal sites and a second assembly line at Cranage Aerodrome from 1941 of more than 1,150 a year and overall roughly equivalent to one for every factory employee at the peak of activity. By the end of 1940, 490 Wellingtons had been built, followed by 897 in 1941, 1,356 in 1942, 1,356 in 1943, 1,217 in 1944, and 224 in 1945 (up to September when production ceased after the completion of the 5,540th aircraft). This total comprised three Mk.I; seventeen Mk. IA; 1,583 Mk. IC; 737 Mk. III; 220 Mk. IV; 2,434 Mk.X; eight tropicalized Mk. XII; and 538 Mk.XIV aircraft. 235 Avro Lancaster heavy bombers and eleven Lincolns were also built between June 1944 and September 1945. The end of the war meant that all aircraft manufactured at this Vickers bastion of big bomber production ceased after a grand total of 5,786 aircraft had been produced in exactly six hectic years – an overall average of more than 1,150 a year.

*The Vickers-Armstrongs Ltd company title together with twin sandstone-carved interlaced 'V-A' logos prominently featured above the main entrance and in the glass doorway panels of the Chester site management and administration block.*

Because of the delay in the ground levelling due to the quagmire and the consequently difficult surface tracking conditions, the contractors' promise to deliver the south-west corner of the main factory site by the third week of February 1939 could not be kept. A Bellman-type hangar was therefore borrowed from the Air Ministry and erected on the edge of the site near the Glynne Arms public house in order to begin assembly of the first aircraft while simultaneously providing on-the-job training of local workpeople.

The first pair of Wellington fuselage assembly jigs and main structural frames in place in the temporary Bellman hangar with geodetic panels available to start construction of the first Chester-built aircraft in April 1939.

40

The first Wellington fuselage assembly jigs installed in the south-west corner of the new factory, the first area to be completed and occupied in mid-June 1939. The partially completed assembly of the first aircraft was then transferred from the Bellman hangar to this area in mid-July alongside the first batch of completed skeletal geodetic fuselage structures.

The first Chester-built Wellington, a Mk.1 L7770, assembled in the four months between the start of work on 3 April 1939 and first flight on 2 August 1939 by 'Mutt' Summers, Vickers chief test pilot, before being delivered to the Royal Air Force just at the outbreak of war on 3 September 1939. This was a remarkable achievement under the guiding hand of Gordon Montgomery, Assembly Manager, with a small team and parts from the Vickers-Weybridge Factory, while working alongside the construction of the main factory and simultaneously training the nucleus of staff for its occupation. Sir Robert McLean, the Chairman of Vickers (Aviation) Ltd (dark suit) and Montgomery (with hat and raincoat) are observing immediately in front of the nose turret.

*Take-off of Wellington L7770 on its first flight on 2 August 1939. Considerable difficulty had been experienced in moving the aircraft out of the unfinished factory and onto the newly constructed Hawarden Aerodrome. This was because the drainage system had not proceeded as quickly as hoped and large areas were under water, leaving only one end available for flying. Consequently, the aircraft had to be flown to Weybridge for full flight clearance. By late 1940, only having laid a single short (700-yd) runway (still used today as a taxiway and known as the 'Vickers Track'), the contractors were hard pressed to build all the facilities that were so badly needed that wet winter.*

*The Vickers patented drawbench machine, incorporating an elaborate cam and roller control mechanism for forming and shaping the multitude of individual geodesic channel members embodied in the Wellington airframe and drawn from aluminium strip and hand-sawn to length. This ingenious machine can be fairly regarded as a forerunner of the modern generation of computer-controlled machine tools. The very high production rate meant that Vickers could afford to tool up the subcontractors to handle all the geodetic rolling mill work and three firms in the Midlands – the Singer Motor Company, Howard and Buller, and Johnson and Barlow – undertook this work for the geodetic construction of the Wellington at Chester.*

# The Geodetic Structural Concept

The unusual geodetic ('basketweave') structural principle deployed so effectively in the Vickers Wellington was the brainchild of the legendary Barnes Wallis and originated in the method that he devised for the retention of the gas-bags of the Vickers R100 airship of 1929. Because of the difficulty in estimating the structural loads, the Airworthiness and Airship Panel would not allow the retention wires to be fixed to the longitudinal beams. Contriving a spirally-wound retaining wire mesh attached to a secondary structure, Wallis sought the guidance of Professor Filon, Professor of Mathematics at University College, London, who advised that the lines required were 'geodesics' and provided the analytical equations.

Geodesy, from which this concept was derived, is a branch of mathematics dealing with the measurement of the shape and surface of the Earth, wherein a 'geodetic line' or 'geodesic' is defined as the shortest distance between two points on a curved surface and known in global navigation as a 'great circle' route. When Wallis joined Rex Pierson, Vickers Chief Designer at Weybridge, as Chief Structural Designer in 1930, he reasoned that this concept could have an analogous meaning in aircraft design by enabling the stresses to be carried by the shortest route in an ideal load-balance and fail-safe combination. It could also replace normal primary and secondary members with a self-stabilising system of main members only, doing the work of the shell of a conventional monocoque, without the need for internal load-carrying structure. Near-ideal streamlined external shapes could thus be adopted, together with maximum unobstructed internal space and high strength and stiffness. Stressed-skinning could also be dispensed with, and well-practised, minimum-weight, fabric covering still be used.

By helical-winding the load-bearing structural members in opposite directions along the length of a substantially single-curvature tubular fuselage, and joining them at each crossover, one set of 'geodetic bars' was in tension while the other was in compression. The resulting curved diagonal lattice, stabilised by quartile tubular longerons, thus lay along the lines in which the principal in-flight forces acted and absorbed all loads by stress equalisation in sustaining the bending, shear and torsional loading generated by the aerodynamic forces on the airframe. As applied to a wing, tailplane or fin, this structural form also afforded exceptional torsional stiffness, allowing a high aspect ratio (for long range), without the tendency to flutter or aileron reversal as with a more conventional design.

First applied to the Vickers G.4/31 biplane prototype of 1934 and its production derivative, the Vickers Wellesley long-range monoplane bomber of 1935, this ingenious, if complex, structural system was fully exploited in the large-scale high-rate production of the Wellington. Axiomatically, completely new design and manufacturing processes were necessary to translate the Wallis concept into practical reality. These imperatives came from the ingenuity and drive of three other Vickers-Weybridge stalwarts. Basil Stephenson, in the design office, was responsible for geometric/spatial definition of the nodal co-ordinates of the lattice structure in relation to the airframe external shape. This permitted the mathematical definition of the unwrapped spiral members in a series of chordal lengths and intersecting angles to be expressed in tabular form. Although Professor A.J. Sutton Pippard of London University provided Wallis with a method of stress analysis, this was not used and Vickers developed its own. Charlie Smith, the toolroom foreman, in conjunction with Jack East, Works Engineer, then brilliantly devised the ingenious strip-rolling machines, using an intricate arrangement of adjustable sets of cams and rollers, to form and shape the multitude of individual channel-section members. The whole concept was then brought into mass production simultaneously in the three Wellington factories – Weybridge, Chester and Blackpool – by the redoubtable Trevor Westbrook. In active service, the geodetic-type construction of the Wellington brought the added bonus of its ability to withstand major battle damage and still enable flight crews to 'get home' safely.

Boiler-plate sheets drilled and pegged to check the profiles of the geodesic members after forming.

Assembly of the geodesic members in diagonal lattice pattern.

Pre-assembled fuselage geodetic panel stores supplied from subcontractors. The Wellington structural skeleton consisted of curved channel-section members ('geodetic bars') laid in opposite directions. Those running in one direction were cut halfway through on the inside of the curve and those running in the other direction were cut on the outer surface – and inter-connected with specially designed machined 'butterfly' and 'wishbone' fittings, rivets and bolts. The bars were then joined to the fuselage stabilzing tubular longerons (or wing spar) by shear cleat and gusset plate attachments.

The first semblance of a Wellington assembly line in the main factory in mid-September 1939, with the second machine nearing completion at the far end of the shop, followed by two lines of fuselages and then a pair of wings. Bottom right: further jig support structures awaiting assembly.

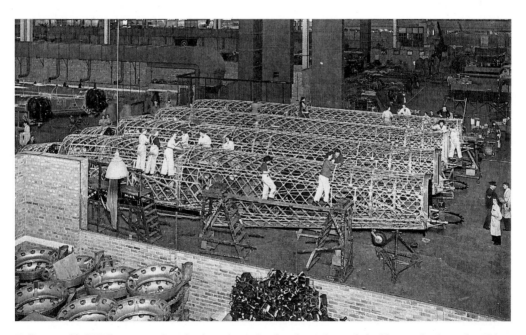

Fully assembled Wellington geodetic fuselages being fitted with overlaying bolted longitudinal wooden 'fabric rails' for the attachment of the Irish Linen fabric covering. The geodetic panels were broken at the longerons for ease of construction, but as the lengths of these longerons were short, the resulting bending moment in them was very small. They took the tension and compression loads due to bending, and the geodetic bars the shear and torsion, while also supporting the longerons against buckling.

Wellington fuselage at an advanced stage of the fabric skin covering. Attachment of this covering to the geodetic structural members was achieved by capping strips screwed to the wooden fabric rails to prevent chafing against the structure and edge-sewn, eight double-cord stitches to the inch. The screws were first bench-fitted to the rails by a near-blind operator who drove around 6,000 screws a day. Each fuselage then incorporated 8,000 small bolts in the fitting of the rails to the airframe.

Background: fabric covering, stitching and dope stretching of Wellington wing structures. For the wings and similar surfaces the fabric was looped around a securing wire reinforcement and stitched through small holes in the outside flange of the geodetic bars, with the stitches being securely knotted on the inside. Foreground: application of identification markings to the bullet-proof, self-sealing, rail-mounted, rubber bladder petrol tanks.

*The Bristol Hercules engine dressing and nacelle ('power egg') assembly area.*

*A visiting RAF aircrew being shown the fabric covering of Wellington tail-planes by (left) Charlie Boon, Chief Inspector (ex-Weybridge).*

*Wellington production for Royal Air Force Coastal Command. Foreground: completed, equipped and fabric-covered fuselages. Centre: fin/rudder and other assemblies. Background right: fuselage/inner wing and power plant assembly, and left: complete aircraft final assembly. The Wellington was the most prolific British two-motor bomber of the Second World War and was in full-scale production at Chester throughout the conflict.*

*Left: Wellington Mk.XIV general reconnaissance version for RAF Coastal Command. Right: Wellington Mk.X trainer (the most prolific variant produced at Chester – 2,434) awaiting delivery. Wellington output from Chester peaked at around 130 aircraft a month (or around 4½ per day, seven days a week). The intensive production test flying at Hawarden was under the control of Maurice Hare who had transferred from Weybridge as Chief Production Test Pilot, and personally flew just over 3,000 aircraft on test at Chester, supported by only a few other ex-Weybridge test pilots and short-stay service pilots.*

# Wellington Production World Record

A dramatic highlight of the prodigious Chester-built Wellington output was a new world record in 1944 for the fastest production assembly of an aircraft, the existing record being set by an American factory, which built a Douglas Boston twin-engined bomber in 48 hours. To boost national morale, the management and workers decided to attempt to assemble and fly a Wellington inside 30 hours of non-stop working. The mission was completed in 24 hours and 48 minutes from the start of assembly to lift-off, little over half the existing time. It was recorded by the Ministry of Information Crown Film Unit in an 18-minute documentary entitled *Workers Weekend – A Tribute to the Workers of the British Aircraft Industry*, narrated by an officer of the Royal Canadian Air Force to give it added authenticity in North America.

The normal works routine at Chester in wartime was 6 a.m. to 11 p.m., seven days a week, and about half of the 6,000 Chester workers were women. Between fifty and sixty workers were selected from the numerous volunteers to make the record attempt. Beginning at 9 a.m. on a Saturday morning, they also undertook to donate the bonus they would earn that day to the Red Cross Aid-to-Russia Fund. The rapid precision-fitting assembly of the main fuselage components and interior frames, systems and equipment resulted in the completed fuselage coming out of jig by 1.45 p.m. for fabric covering and the application of nine coats of quick-drying, fabric-stretching and weather-proofing dope. Assembly of the complete airframe – with wings, petrol tanks, tail unit surfaces, bomb-beam and engine/nacelle 'power-eggs' that had been simultaneously pre-assembled and delivered from elsewhere in the factory – was complete by 6.15 p.m.. The nightshift started at 8 p.m., the propellers, gun turrets and landing gear were fitted by 10.30 p.m., the RAF roundels painted on at 3 a.m. on Sunday morning, and the aircraft was towed from the assembly line to the engine-running shed 20 minutes later. By 6.15 a.m., 21 hours and 15 minutes into the record attempt, the aircraft was a complete fighting unit and saw the first dawn of its lifetime. After two hours of final adjustments and inspection, the fully assembled, equipped, checked and tested aircraft was rolled out onto the airfield ready for take-off at 8.50 a.m., just ten minutes short of a day. With ex-RAF test pilot, Gerald Whinney, at the controls, Chester-built Wellington Mk.X LN514, lifted off the Hawarden Aerodrome after just 24 hours and 48 minutes of non-stop working from the start of the assembly and almost halved the world-record time for the fastest construction time for a bomber aircraft. At 7.45 p.m. it was flown by a ferry pilot to its operational base.

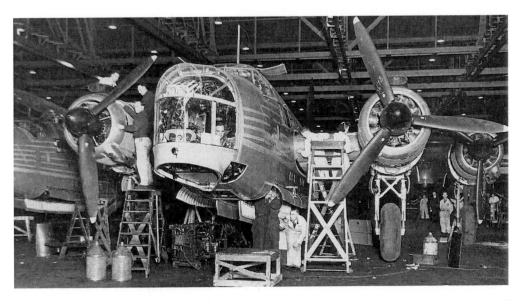

# Wartime Royal Visits

Above: HM King George VI, *appropriately dressed in Royal Air Force uniform, and Queen Elizabeth (the Queen Mother of today) visiting the Chester Factory on 15 July 1942 escorted by Bernard Duncan, Superintendent. The Wellington Mk. III BJ708, which they saw take off, was delivered to No.38 Maintenance Unit (MU) RAF at Llandow the following day, before being issued to No.75 Squadron, but was lost on operations on 27 August 1942.*

*The first wartime Royal visit was by HRH The Duke of Kent, then an RAF Group Captain, who made a tour of the RAF Hawarden camp and No.7 Operational Training Unit (OTU) on 24 September 1940. He made a second visit on 7 May 1942.*

Left: HM King George VI *taking a keen interest in the work of Olive North, one of the many skilled female workers at Chester, on the assembly of the Wellington front fuselage and nose gun turret ring.*

# The Broughton Wellington

'The Broughton Wellington' Mk. IC R1333 – proudly bearing the Welsh Red Dragon emblem and inscription under the cockpit – on 7 November 1940. It was presented to the Royal Air Force through donations from the 'Workers and Co-operators' of Vickers-Chester, the Bristol Aeroplane Company (for the Pegasus engines) and their then 350 subcontractors. Together, they had donated £15,300 of the total cost of £20,000 with Vickers Ltd subscribing the balance of £4,700 (at a time when average shop floor weekly earnings were around £2.10s (£2.50).

In the letter to Lord Beaverbrook, the ebullient Minister of Aircraft Production, which accompanied the cheque, Duncan wrote, 'There is a natural desire that the gift should take the form of a particular Wellington allotted to an operational squadron soon after completion at the factory; also that it should be known as 'The Broughton Wellington' and the aircraft about to commence assembly at these works under the serial number R1333 should be the chosen one. By this means we should be able to keep the subscribers informed of some operations in which the aircraft took part and so maintain interest and enthusiasm.' However, despite this most commendable gesture, the aircraft did not actually see active service. After transfer to No.48 MU on the Hawarden Aerodrome, and being damaged during the air raid directed at Coventry on 14 November 1940, a week after the hand-over, it was delivered to 99 Squadron at Newmarket, Cambridgeshire, on 1 December 1940. Unfortunately it crashed there on take-off on 18 December and was burnt out, killing the rear gunner. A replacement aircraft of the same name, R1516, was delivered to the No.311 (Czecho-Slovak) Squadron and later also lost on operations.

*Naming 'The Broughton Wellington' on 7 November 1940. Left to right: Tommy Lucke, Vickers Test Pilot; Gordon Montgomery, Works Manager; Bernard Duncan, Superintendent; and Miss Scott, a senior secretary who had worked at Vickers House in London before the war, who cut the ribbon.*

# Other Notable Chester-Built Wellingtons

Wellington Mk. IC R1296, built at Chester in late 1940, which featured in the famous cinematograph film *Target for Tonight*, produced by the Crown Film Unit with the full co-operation of the Royal Air Force. Every member of the cast was played by actual members of the service carrying out their normal duties.

It was the Chester-built Wellington Mk. IC, L7818, on which Sergeant James Allen Ward, of No.75 (New Zealand) Squadron and second pilot of the aircraft, won the Victoria Cross on the night of 7 July 1941. Returning from an attack on Munster in Germany, the aircraft was attacked from beneath by a Messerschmitt 110 night fighter, setting fire to the starboard engine. Courageously, Ward crawled along the wing, kicking footholes in the fabric, and smothered the fire with an engine cover. By this heroic action, he enabled the aircraft to get home safely.

Chester Factory workers must have been dismayed to learn that one of their aircraft, L7788, which crash-landed in Holland, was repaired and flown in German Luftwaffe markings!

Wellington T.Mk.X LN715, originally built at Chester and later adapted to be powered by the Rolls-Royce Dart propeller-turbine engines in association with the development of the Vickers Viscount, Britain's most successful post-war airliner, and first flown in this configuration on 10 June 1948.

To help maintain the required Wellington production rate at the Chester Factory, in 1941 it became necessary to open a satellite assembly plant at Byley, twenty-five miles to the east, near Middlewich in mid-Cheshire, and to the south-west of the Cranage Aerodrome (by which name the plant was always known). The large grass airfield there was originally built to accommodate RAF No.2 School of Air Navigation from October 1940 but was later adapted for fighter squadrons and used as a main line of defence for Merseyside. The first Cranage Wellington was completed in September of that year. This general view of the exterior of the Byley facility is fronted by a large number of fuselage transport dollies and aircraft jacks.

The Wellington flight shed, some fields away from the Cranage Aerodrome – to where the many hundreds of aircraft produced at the main works at Byley were towed along the interconnecting taxiway for preparation for flight and delivery.

*Operating as a mass-production assembly plant only, with the manufacture of all components being subcontracted, the Chester Factory and the Cranage satellite relied on a number of other local supporting dispersal sites to facilitate this process. These twin gable-ended hangar examples at Aston Hall – camouflaged to resemble agricultural barns – were replicated at Dobs Hill, Ewloe and Kinnerton.*

*Pre-assembly of the fabric-covered geodetic tailplanes and flying control surfaces at the Anchor Motors garage in Chester and typifying the multitude of small local subcontractors supporting the Chester and Cranage Wellington assembly lines. Test flying at the Hawarden and Cranage airfields – led by ex-naval officer, Maurice Hare as Chief Test Pilot, together with other Vickers and short-stay RAF test pilots – was relatively uneventful except for the tragic loss of the Wellington X HE819 at Cranage. Landing from its third test flight, the port wing touched the ground causing the aircraft to swing round, break up and burst into flames, killing Flying Officer Rouff, a South African test pilot, and Edward Booth, a Vickers inspector.*

Foreground: the last batch of Vickers Wellington fuselage production. Background: the first Vickers-built Avro 683 Lancaster B.Mk.1 four-engined heavy bombers in final assembly at Chester.

Right foreground: Wellington final assembly line with (upper left) Avro Lancaster assembly line.

*Wickman and Asquith machines in the Lancaster wing-spar milling shop. Vickers-Chester became responsible for construction of the centre wing/fuselage component for the Lancasters built there but with other major components being supplied by Avro's own main supply sources, notably Chadderton and Yeadon.*

*Lancaster centre wing-spar assembly.*

Lancaster centre wing and fuselage section assembly in the West Annexe. The conventional stressed-skin, monocoque-type fuselage structure and Warren-braced twin-spar wing construction of this aircraft was in total contrast to the geodetic-type structure of the Vickers Wellington.

Lancaster nose fuselage sections – incorporating the prone bomb-aiming, nose gun turret and cockpit windows. Roy Chadwick, the renowned Avro Chief Designer, had deliberately designed the Lancaster airframe to be broken down into large fully equipped and road-transportable sections for ease and speed of dispersed production. (This method is common practice today, notably with international programmes such as the Airbus family, but now with fast long-distance aerial transport rather than the then shorter-distance road transport.)

57

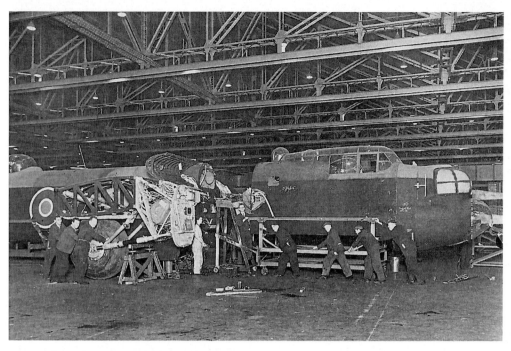

*Mating of Lancaster nose and main fuselage sections.*

*Lancaster mainplane and control surface assembly.*

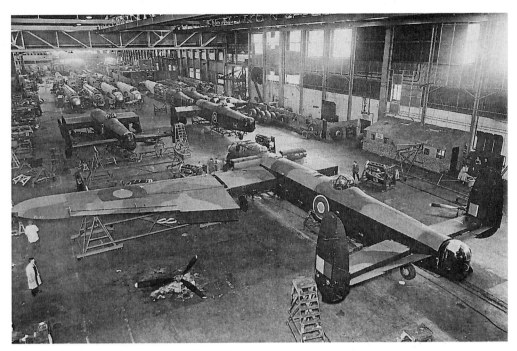

*Lancaster assembly line. Foreground: inner wing-to-centre wing/fuselage join-up. Centre: rear fuselage/centre wing assemblies. Background: Wellington fuselages undergoing fabric covering and internal equipping.*

*Lancasters nearing completion and transfer to the adjoining engine running shed.*

*Upper right: Lancaster assembly line paralleling continuing assembly of the Wellington. Vickers produced its first Lancaster in June 1944 and its 235th and last in August 1945, during which period a peak of thirty-six aircraft a month was reached.*

*The Avro Lincoln derivative of the Lancaster, originally known as the Lancaster IV and designed for operation against the Japanese. The abrupt ending of the Far East conflict in August 1945 meant that the Lincoln did not see action in the Second World War. Eleven of these Avro 'super-bombers' were assembled at Chester between June and August 1945 (together with the last twenty-three Chester-built Lancasters) from components supplied by Metropolitan Vickers at Trafford Park, Manchester. These were the last batch of the prodigious output of 5,786 aircraft to be built at Chester in exactly six years under the Vickers-Armstrongs management.*

# Three

# The Blackpool Sibling

The second Vickers Wellington Shadow Factory was located at Squires Gate airport on the Southern outskirts of Blackpool on the Fylde coast of Lancashire. Although operating completely autonomously, it had many similarities to that at Chester. Owned by the Government and operated by Vickers-Armstrongs, it was opened in 1940 and from October 1941 had a secondary assembly line at the Stanley Park Municipal Airport to the north-east of the town. However, unlike Chester, which was an assembly works only, Blackpool was laid out as a modern duplicate of the parent factory at Weybridge to manufacture the aircraft complete in all details. The entire aircraft output during the Vickers-Armstrongs management consisted of Wellingtons and totalled 3,406 aircraft, the first being completed in July 1940 and the last in October 1945. Eight were built between September the end of 1940, 199 during 1941, 615 in 1942, 930 in 1943, 1,125 in 1944, and 529 by October 1945, when production finally ceased. The Type breakdown was: fifty Mk. IC; 780 Mk. III; 1369 Mk.X; seventy-five Mk.XI; 802 Mk.XIII; 250Mk.XIV; and eighty Mk.XVIII. Again, as at Chester, 11,250 prefabricated houses were built by the Blackpool unit between September 1945 and April 1948, before Vickers finally vacated the plant in October 1949.

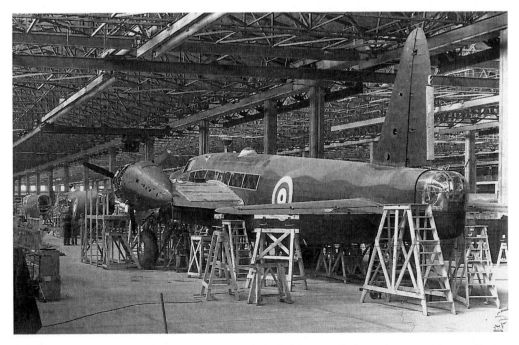

*Wellington final assembly at the Vickers-Blackpool Shadow Factory built on the original historic Squires Gate Aerodrome.*

The massive machine shop at Blackpool, producer of the huge number of machined fittings used in the Wellington geodetic structural panel assemblies. It was estimated that each Wellington airframe incorporated 2,800 cross-over gussets and 'butterfly' fittings, 650 longeron gussets and 'wishbone' fittings, and 35,000 rivets. For the three-factory total of 11,460 aircraft built, and assuming the equivalent of a further 1,000 airframes for spares and repairs, means that the overall totals of the three types of fastenings were approximately 35 million; 8.125 million and 4.375 billion respectively. These figures do not include special rivets/bolts in the main supporting structural framework and engine nacelles which could have increased the count by at least another 10 per cent.

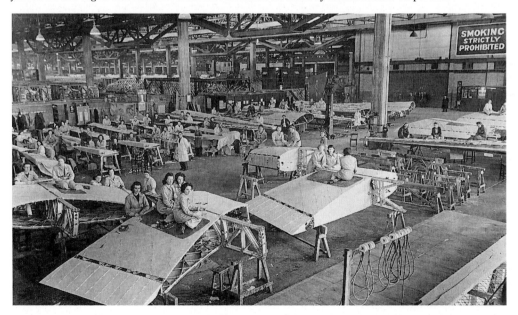

The Wellington inner and outer wing fabric covering, stitching and doping area at the Blackpool works, populated exclusively by female workers as they were presumed especially adept at this tailoring-like work.

# Highlights of the Blackpool Shadow Factory

Alex Dunbar, General Manager of the Vickers Aircraft Section, decided on the location of the Vickers Wellington Shadow Factory at Blackpool after sites at Exeter and Doncaster had been studied. The Air Ministry contract for the construction and equipping of the new unit by the Ministry of Aircraft Production was issued on 30 December 1939, and the first sod cut on 3 January 1940. The Squires Gate Aerodrome, on which the factory was built, was the scene of a famous flying meeting in October 1909 organised by Lord Northcliffe, proprietor of the Daily Mail (giving the present airport a longer history than any other in Britain). With good approaches and flat surroundings, at the outbreak of the Second World War it was seen as a good base for RAF Coastal Command. As at Chester, Wellington production began in a Bellman hangar on the edge of the airfield, pending completion of the Shadow Factory. Started from Weybridge and not from Chester, as might be supposed, the first contract was for 500 Wellingtons, the first aircraft was rolled out in July 1940 and the first three production machines were delivered by the end of that month.

The factory was much bigger than Chester, and had its own machine shops and subcontractors. Production dispersal depots were opened in the area, including the Harrowside Bridge and Belle Vue garages, the Talbot and Devonshire Road bus depots, the Whitegate Drive tram depot and St. John's Market Hall. A secondary assembly line at Stanley Park was established on 26 October 1941.

A shortage of skilled labour was partly overcome by the transfer of personnel from the Vickers shipyard at Barrow-in-Furness. However, a serious hold-up in the production programme occurred on 9 August 1940. After the completion of the construction of the main works, the centre-section of the main aircraft erection bay collapsed, killing six men outright and injuring thirteen others, one fatally. The resulting disruption had a serious effect on the output of aircraft. The bombing and serious disruption of the Vickers-Weybridge Factory a month later meant the MAP also instructed Vickers to disperse the test flying of all its experimental aircraft types to Blackpool. When full production resumed, a rate of fifteen to twenty aircraft a week was reached. At one time a contract was received for the production of 300 Vickers Warwick aircraft, but shortly afterwards cancelled. The manufacture of 11,250 AIROH prefabricated houses, the same number as at Chester, superseded that of aircraft. The first was completed in September 1945 and the contract completed in April 1948 – when the factory was finally vacated by Vickers on 18 October 1949 before resuming aircraft production for a period during the early 1950s by Hawkers with the Hunter jet fighter.

*The administrative arrangements at Blackpool were generally similar to those at Chester. Seen here with the one-thousandth Blackpool-built Wellington ready for delivery in 1942 are, left to right: Frank White (Subcontract Manager), Les Webb (Production Manager), Pat Molony (Works Manager), Sam Bower (Superintendent throughout the period of production by Vickers), Ernie Comley (Personnel Manager), and Teddy Major (Chief Inspector).*

*Vickers Wellington geodetic fuselage structures in progressive stages of completion at the Blackpool Squires Gate Shadow Factory.*

*Wellington wing production and fabric covering exhibiting the same kind of geodetic construction as the fuselage and other fixed flying control surfaces.*

*Wellington component sub-assembly manufacturing area showing, bottom to top: inner wings, control surfaces and outer wings, fuselages, and, top right: fuselage equipping and skinning.*

*Prototype Vickers Wellington MK.IV R1220 built at Chester but seen here outside one of the two camouflaged shallow 'V' clerestory roofed hangers at Squires Gate (as seen on page 67) to where this aircraft had been flown for experimantal flight-testing.*

*A Blackpool-built, Bristol Hercules-powered, Vickers Wellington T.MK.XVIII NC869 fitted with a de Havilland Mosquito nose and modified to house a radar scanner for training night-fighter crews.*

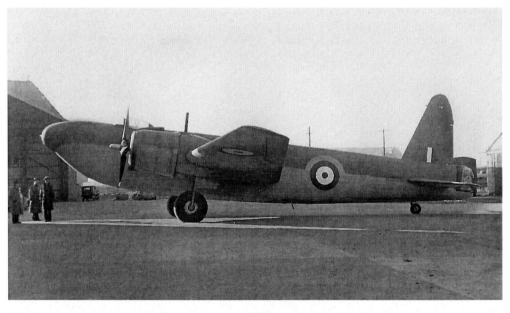

*The first prototype pressurised-cabin, high-altitude Wellington Mk.V R3298, which was flown from the Vickers-Weybridge Factory to Blackpool on 25 September 1940. After the disastrous bombing of the vulnerable Brooklands Factory and airfield on 4 September 1940, the Government insisted that all test flying of Vickers experimental aircraft types be transferred to Squires Gate. However, it was not until late October 1940 that high-altitude flight up to 30,000ft and beyond was possible due to icing of the pilot's canopy dome.*

*The last Blackpool-built Wellington T.10 Trainer, RP590, and the very last of the 11,460 production Wellingtons built at Weybridge, Chester and Blackpool, making a final salute to the Squires Gate Factory prior to being handed over to the Royal Air Force on 25 October 1945. (RAF Museum/Charles E. Brown Collection (6083-7))*

# The Blackpool Wellington Legacy

Most notable among the 3,406 Wellingtons built at the Blackpool Shadow Factory was Wellington Mk.X MF628 which, after a distinguished active display career, is today the only surviving complete Vickers Wellington and is displayed in the Bomber Command Collection at the Royal Air Force Museum at Hendon, North London. First flown at Blackpool on 9 May 1944, MF628 was initially allotted to No.18 Maintenance Unit (MU) RAF, at Dumfries, Scotland, on 11 May 1944 before being modified to T.Mk X standard by Boulton and Paul in 1948. Damaged during service as a navigational trainer, after a ten-month repair by Brooklands Aviation at Sywell, Northamptonshire, between December 1951 and October 1952, it was tranferred to 19 MU RAF at St Athan, South Wales, before taking part in the 'Fifty Years of Flying' display at the Royal Aeronautical Society's (RAeS) Garden Party at de Havilland Hatfield on 14 June 1953.

After flying over Lake Windermere in August 1954 to appear in the film, *The Dambusters*, MF628 was sold to Vickers-Armstrongs at Weybridge on 24 January 1955 and flown from St Athan to Wisley in the last ever Wellington flight. Vickers then presented the aircraft to the RAeS at the Society's Garden Party at Wisley on 15 July 1956. After several more moves during the next six years, this historic aircraft was handed over by the RAeS on permanent loan to the Ministry of Defence in mid-1964. Refurbished to display standard at St Athan, and exhibited at RAF Abingdon before HM The Queen on 14 June 1968 to commemorate the fiftieth anniversary of the RAF, MF628 was ultimately moved on 26 October 1971 to its current proud resting place at the RAF Museum at Hendon. The only other surviving Wellington, and the only one to have seen operational service during the Second World War is the Weybridge-built aircraft N2980 'R for Robert' that was dramatically recovered from Loch Ness in Scotland on 21 September 1985. It has since been splendidly restored and preserved at the Brooklands Museum with the partly covered airframe readily exhibiting the distinctive geodetic type construction.

# Four

# From Bomber to Bungalow

## A Peace Dividend

During the Second World War, the manpower in the house-building sector diminished dramatically as the personnel were required in the armed forces and the war industries, and later to repair bomb-damaged homes. By the end of the war, timber and bricks were in short supply, meaning a serious delay in the building of much needed conventional homes. This prompted the preparation of an AIROH (Aircraft Industry Research on Housing) pre-fabricated aluminium and concrete house design for large-scale production as a temporary solution to the housing deficit.

The Vickers shadow factories at Chester and Blackpool were each contracted by the Government to build 11,250 of these ingenious constructions. The conversion of aircraft factories for the construction of these 'prefabs' was a major undertaking but expeditiously fulfilled. Moreover, the utility of this radically different output provided a vital continuity in employment as well as a valuable contribution to the regeneration of peacetime Britain. More than 150,000 of these homes were built and erected nationwide, with funding and materials from the US as part of the post-war Marshall Aid Plan. Valued at £1,200 each in 1947, they were typically rented at fifteen shillings per week, and those remaining might well now sell for £35,000.

*A typical AIROH utilitarian-design, cottage-style pre-fabricated home, fully assembled, equipped and occupied. Each unit was built in modular form and comprised a living room, two bedrooms, fitted kitchen (not previously seen in the UK, with worktops in pressed steel and cream and green enamel), bathroom, toilet, and hall. Each had a front entrance, the internal doors connected directly with the hall, with the exception of the kitchen which was entered either from the living room or from outside.*

*A corner of the foam cement plant with the cement silo fronted by the receiving building.*

*The partition wall casting platform in the foam cement plant. The outer walls were sandwiched between two sheets of light alloy and baked cement.*

*Internal partition wall plasterboard application area and upending gear in the foam cement plant.*

*Foreground: the partition wall undercoat paint plant with the dripping and draining tanks. The production line moved at 1½ft per minute. (This process plant was an interesting portent of the huge completely automated Airbus wing skin panel treatment plant that was installed at Broughton during 1999.)*

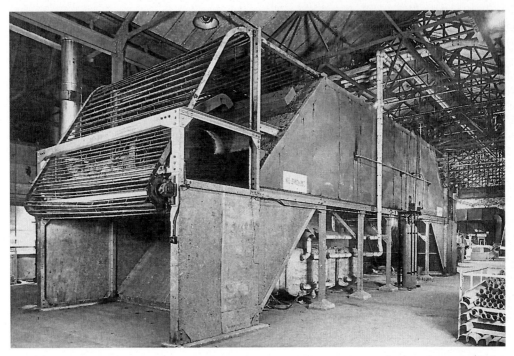

*The kitchen and bathroom unit (KBU) stoving oven, typifying the large-scale specialised machinery that had to be installed for the production of pre-fabricated houses instead of aircraft*

*Floor assembly in the south and main shop floor areas of the Chester Factory, indicating the value of adaptation of the extensive overhead crane rails originally installed for the movement of large aircraft components.*

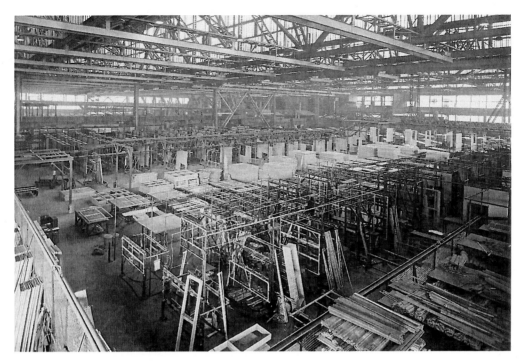

*Wall assembly with an immense amount of materials being handled.*

*Assembly of the Warren-braced hip roof support modules.*

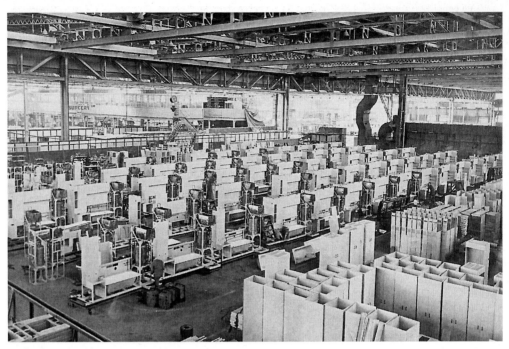

*Assembly of the modular KBU and cupboard unit structures.*

*Kitchen side of the finished KBU with a modern, space-efficient fitted kitchen, with oven and gas refrigerator. This unit was an integral back-to-back module separating the two rooms of the dwelling.*

*Bathroom side of the KBU with; right: built-in lagged main and hot water tanks.*

*KBU module assembly lines, with floor, and, foreground: wall and external window frame installations moving on wheeled platforms and floor track runners for automobile-style line production.*

*Attachment of the roof structures using a 'Kings' overhead hoist.*

*Main assembly lines (kitchen side of the KBU), moving towards attachment of the roof modules and into the final external treatment process chambers.*

*Assembled house modules moving into the external treatment process chambers.*

*One of the four fully equipped ex-works house modules being loaded for transport by contract carrier to the erection site. Each house left the factory in four sections, completely equipped and painted, on their own trailers. Seven men could then erect it in two hours on a pre-prepared foundation. A few hours were then required for the connection of public utilities.*

*Despatch area with house sections loaded with temporary hessian transport covers at the open ends.*

*Prefabricated house section leaving the Chester Factory site past the main canteen and works transport building. By the end of 1945, a few of these ingenious and fully functional domestic dwellings had been built by hand methods but production quickly gather momentum and a maximum weekly output of 170 complete units was soon reached. The full production run of 11,250 units was completed in April 1948. Originally intended to last only 10 to 15 years, hundreds remain in occupation today, more then 60 years after they were originally built, which speaks volumes for both the original concept and the quality of the ex-aircraft workmanship. In 1998, several surviving prefab housing sites were given Grade II listing for posterity by English Heritage, notably a row of 16 at Wake Green in the Hall Green superb of Birmingham, installed in 1946-47, still occupied and little changed, apart from modern-style windows and a heating system. In 2004, the Stafford Borough Council's refurbishment of council-owned prefabs found the substructure in good condition when the aluminium cladding was renewed with modern-day cladding designed to simulate traditional brick-built walls. This notably led to one being saved by an enthusiastic individual owner and this type of building not having been designated as defective under Part XVI of the Housing Act 1984. In March 2005, a two-bedroom prefab, empty for 15 years, was auctioned for an astonishing £277,000, principally for its location – in Bristol's Sneyd Park where houses often sell for more than £1 million. That same year, 60 years on, Bristol City Council began to replace all its 350 prefabs on 15 sites. A cluster of 180 prefabs also remains on the Excalibur Estate at Catford in south-east London.*

*Five*

# The de Havilland Dynasty

The availability of the Chester facility in 1948 enabled the de Havilland Aircraft Company (DH) to fulfil the burgeoning export order-book for its Vampire jet fighter and Dove light transport aircraft. It became the the main outlet for all designs in the prolific DH dynasty during the next 12 years of the company's operation of the factory. For five years from 1960 the DH name continued on the masthead under the Hawker Siddeley regime as the HS de Havilland Division. The open-plan floor enabled large-scale production lines of numerous types to be handled simultaneously. The transfer of the completed units to the pre-flight area was made via the inherited factory-wide overhead craneage system. However the smaller Chipmunk and Beaver and the larger, more complex and slower-moving Comet jetliner were built on conventional nose-to-tail and herringbone assembly lines. 3,532 aircraft of eight DH types were produced between mid-1948 and the end of 1959 – Mosquito (65), Hornet (149), Vampire and Vampire Trainer (1,236), Chipmunk (889), Dove (209), Venom (834), Heron (129) and Comet (13).

*The new DH name above the entrance to the Chester site management and administration block in 1948, with the twin sandstone-carved interlocked 'V-A' (Vickers-Armstrongs) logos of its predecessor still in situ.*

Assembly at Chester of the first laminated wooden ('pea-pod') fuselage half-shells for the famous DH 98 Mosquito fighter-bomber (which was dubbed 'The Wooden Wonder') in mid-May 1948. The Mosquito was the first DH manufacturing programme to be undertaken there and was the end phase of the overall Mosquito production run. The Chester output consisted of eighty-two N.F.Mk.38 Night Fighters and fourteen T.R.Mk.37 Sea Mosquitoes completed between September 1948 and November 1950. Most of the former were for Yugoslavia. The latter version served with 703 Squadron at Solent area bases and provided the Naval Flight of the RAF's Air-Sea Warfare Development Unit. In later years, the Aircraft Repair and Overhaul Organisation (AROO) notably maintained and supported the company-owned Mosquito T III RR299 (G-ASKH) which was, for a long period, regarded as a 'Broughton Trademark' until sadly lost at Barton, near Oldham (the original Manchester airport from 1930 to 1938), on 21 July 1966. Found in storage at Chester in 1952, the prototype Mosquito, first flown on 25 November 1940, is now preserved at its Salisbury Hall birthplace.

VT670, the first Chester-built Mosquito N.F.Mk.38 taxiing past the last of the Vickers Wellingtons for its first flight from the Hawarden Aerodrome on 30 September 1948. The last Chester-built Mosquito was VX916, an N.F.Mk.38, which was first flown on 15 November 1950 and was the 7,781st and last ever example of this extraordinarily successful aircraft.

The DH 103 Hornet production line at Chester in 1950, after the jigs had been transferred from Hatfield towards the end of 1948, and of which type 149 were built at Chester between 1949 and 1952, the last being the seventy-eighth and final Sea Hornet N.F.Mk.21 VZ699 in June 1952. The sleek single-seat Hornet was the world's fastest piston-engined aircraft (485mph) and was intended for use in the Japanese campaign but did not see war service. It was also the RAF's last piston-engined fighter to see service. While the fuselage was of similar construction to the Mosquito, the wing was of composite construction with a double upper skin of plywood and an under-skin of light alloy, with composite wooden spars, assembled in what became known as the 'Redux' bonding process – which featured widely in subsequent all-metal DH designs.

A major spares organisation for the whole of the DH civil and military aircraft family was set up at Chester in 1950, with a world-wide distribution network. A service department was also established there to handle factory repair and overhaul of military aircraft and provide after-sales service to some of the civil aircraft customers. This was later complemented by a nucleus design staff to deal with the customisation of civil aircraft.

The first Chester-built DH100 Vampire twin-boom jet fighter, an FB.5 (with DH production serial V-0080, later registered VZ841) being rolled out for flight testing prior to delivery to the RAF on 30 March 1951 Top left: Mosquitos and top right: Hornets, in front of the Chester flight shed awaiting delivery. This variant became the most common in RAF service, changing the Vampire's role from one of intercepter, to support ground-attack fighter-bomber. Many squadrons were stationed with the Second Tactical Air Force (TAF) in Germany.

Front row: pre-delivery line-up in early 1951 of the last three Hornets built at Chester; middle row: DHC.1 Chipmunk fully aerobatic pilot trainers for the RAF; bottom left: Vampires of an evaluation batch for Norway. Chester-built Chipmunks were exported to over fourteen overseas air arms.

Production of Vampire cockpit/nose stressed-skin fuselage sections with laminated cedar plywood-balsa-plywood carapace shell structures cemented under pressure, in the form of the fuselages of the pre-war DH91 Albatross airliner and the wartime Mosquito. Many Vampire fuselages were built by Fairey Aviation at Heaton Chapel, Stockport, Cheshire, and transported by road to Chester for completion.

Assembly of the Vampire cockpit/nose undercarriage and gun bay to the centre fuselage/wing section.

*Large-scale production of the DH112 Vampire Night Fighter NF.25. Upper left: the DHC.1 Chipmunk assembly line. Chester contributed the largest output of the 4,366 Vampires produced by twelve manufacturers in the UK, Australia, France, India, Italy and Switzerland. Of the 3,269 Vampires built in the UK, Chester built a total of 1,244 of all types between 1949 and 1963: J28.B for Sweden (297); FB.5 (87); FB.9 (705); NF.10 (55); FB.52 (114); FB.54 (12) and 424 T.11 and T.55 Trainers. The Vampire was the first British aircraft to exceed 500mph.*

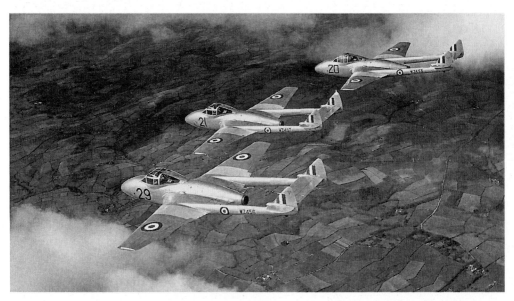

*Chester-built Vampire T.11 Trainers WZ456, WZ457 and WZ453, some of the most widely used advanced jet fighter trainers. The T.11 became the standard jet trainer of the RAF and the Royal Navy. The T.55 version was supplied from Chester to more than twenty air forces: Austria, Burma, Ceylon, Chile, Egypt, Eire, Finland, India, Indonesia, Iraq, Italy, Japan, Lebanon, New Zealand, Norway, South Africa, Sweden, Switzerland, Syria and Venezuela. 117 Vampires were refurbished there. The RAF continued with the type until 1970 and the Swiss Air Force until 1992.*

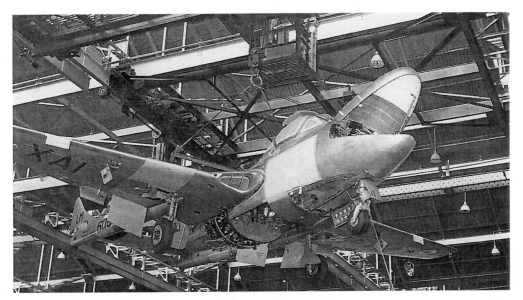

*Vampire Trainer being transported from the Chester main assembly hall to the paint shop and flight preparation area on a 7½-ton 'Royce' overhead crane.*

*DH112 Venom N.F.Mk.2 night fighters – using the basic Venom single-seat airframe with a two-seat side-by-side airframe and AI (airborne interception) radar in an extended nose – on the Hawarden Aerodrome awaiting delivery to No.23 Squadron Royal Air Force at Coltishall, Norfolk. The Venom fighter-bomber, night fighter and Sea Venom constituted the second generation of the distinctive DH twin-boom formula – chosen to shorten the jet tailpipe and reduce power losses from the relatively primitive jet engines then under development. The more powerful DH Ghost engine replaced the DH Goblin and Rolls-Royce Nene of the Vampire. Chester also built sixty-two Venom NF.51s, known as J.33s, with Fairey at Ringway, Manchester, between 1952 and 1957 for the Royal Swedish Air Force. They had Ghost engines, produced under licence in Sweden by Svenska Flygmotor as the RM2A and shipped to Chester for installation.*

*Final assembly of some of the ninety-nine Sea Venom F.A.W. Mk.21s built at Chester in 1955 and 1956. WL813, one of the seventy-three Venom F.B.Mk.4s, made the first air firings of the DH Firestreak guided missile at Aberporth, destroying a Fairey Firefly drone in the process. The Mk.21, XG607, then conducted the service trials of the missile with No.700 Naval Trials Squadron at Ford, Hampshire. Three Chester-built Mk.21s were used for the Royal Navy firing trials which began in December 1958 when three Sea Venom F.A.W Mk.21s were catapulted from HMS Victorious in the Mediterranean in preparation for the introduction of the Firestreak on the succeeding Sea Vixen aircraft, recording 80 per cent direct hits on Malta-based Fireflies.*

*WD327, the 147th Chester-built DHC.1 Chipmunk pilot trainer for the RAF returning from a test flight. It was designed as a successor to the venerable DH82 Tiger Moth, and adopted for the Royal Air Force Volunteer Reserve (RAFVR) flying schools to Specification 8/48 as the T.Mk10. The export demand, with the RAF order for 740 aircraft, was large enough to justify production in the UK for those countries which found it easier to pay in Sterling. UK production of 1,000 Chipmunks was begun in 1949 at Hatfield where 111 were built; the rest were built at Chester, the 1,000th (WZ864) coming off the line on 25 February 1956. A number were also finished by a subcontractor, Hooton Aero Engineering, at nearby Hooton Park.*

*Centre: large-scale refurbishment of RAF Vampire Trainers in 1955 – hence the apparently random serials. Right: the Royal Navy Sea Venom production track. Chester refurbished 177 Vampires between 1954 and 1964, and handled eighty-seven Venom overhauls/resales between 1964 and 1968. 1,241 aircraft were overhauled, refurbished and repaired between 1952 and 1971.*

*Chester-built Chipmunks WK612, WP863, and WP836 over their principal Alma Mater, the renowned Royal Air Force College at Cranwell, Lincolnshire.*

*Royal choice: HRH Prince Charles learning to fly in August 1968 at RAF Tangmere, Sussex, in the Chester-built Day-Glo red Chipmunk T.10 WP903 of The Queen's Flight, under the instruction of Sqn Ldr Philip Pinney of New Zealand serving with the RAF Central Flying School at Little Rissington. Charles received his 'wings' in March 1969. HRH Prince Philip had learned to fly at White Waltham with Chester-built Chipmunks WP861 and WP912, going solo in the latter, now preserved at the RAF Museum Cosford, Shropshire, on 20 December 1952, and using WP912 shortly thereafter and WF848 in 1954/55. Quickly becoming a proficient pilot on the Chipmunk, Prince Philip progressed to the Chester-built twin- and four-engined DH Dove and Heron and other aircraft. WP903 was used by Prince Philip and then for instructional flying by the Duke of Kent, Prince Michael of Kent and the late Prince William of Gloucester. In early 1979, WP904 was used to teach Prince Andrew for his Royal Naval Pilot Graduation.*

*A Chester-built Dove in military guise as the Royal Air Force Devon C.Mk.2 VP978 which served successively with the British Air Attaché in Teheran, Communications Flight in Iraq, Air Attaché in Saigon, conversion to a C.Mk.2, with Nos 21 and 26 Squadrons (temporarily carrying the civil registration G-ALYO when serving on Air Attache duties) and typifying the versatility of the adaptation of the civil Dove to serve in foreign capitals with both the RAF and the Royal Navy (as the Devon and Sea Devon respectively).*

Final assembly of the DH104 Dove light twin-engined transport in 1955 – one of six different DH aircraft types in high-rate production at Chester at that time. So popular was the Dove that production continued there for 17 years, from 1951 to 1967, and to a total of 244 units. They were all powered by successive versions of the DH Gypsy Queen engine, and saw service throughout the world – in civil operation with airlines, business companies and individual owners; and in Government and military service with airforce and naval VIP and staff transport arms.

Personal choice: the specially adapted Chester-built Chipmunk G-APOY (ex-RAF WZ867), owned by the Airways Aero Association and piloted by (later Sir) Peter G. Masefield. It was one of four such aircraft modified in 1959 for civil operation by Bristol Aircraft at Filton (Bristol) at his instigation whilst managing director of the company. It incorporated a single-piece canopy (similar to that of the DH Canada-built Chipmunk T.Mk20 for the Royal Canadian Air Force), navigation beacon and wheel spats. He owned and used a similar aircraft (registered G-AOTM 'Tango Mike') to commute between his home at Reigate, Surrey, from the nearby Croydon, Gatwick and Redhill airfields and the Filton Factory Airfield. Many ex-Service Chipmunks still fly in private hands. The ex-RAF Chipmunk WB975 (the first Chester-built aircraft) and WK520 were returned to Chester for use by the HSA Flying Club.

*Dove production for the Royal New Zealand Navy and North American customers. The Chester Dove production output made a valuable contribution to the national export drive during the 1950s and 1960s. Mid-right: DH Ghost jet engines for Vampire/Venom production.*

*Dove Series 8 G-AREA served successively with Hawker Siddeley Aviation and British Aerospace from 1965 – as did G-ARBE and G-ASMG. G-AREA notably served as the company's Hatfield–Chester shuttle aircraft and is now preserved at the de Havilland Heritage Centre at London Colney, Hertfordshire.*

*Series production at Chester of the enlarged four-engined derivative of the Dove – the DH114 Heron fourteen to seventeen seat feeder-liner – forming a modern successor to the pre-war DH 86 four-engined biplane transport. After the first seven Herons had been built at Hatfield, the last being the prototype Heron 2 with a retractable undercarriage, the production line was transferred to Chester, where 140 Herons were built for VIP, commercial and military service between 1953 and 1967.*

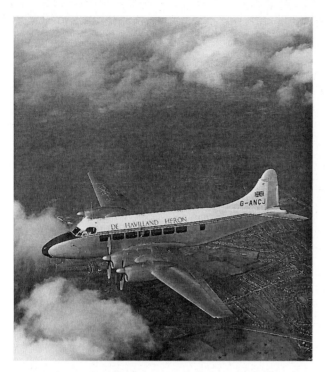

Chester-built Heron 2 G-ANCJ powered by DH Gypsy Queen Series 30 Mk.2 un-supercharged engines and used as a de Havilland sales demonstration and company transport aircraft. The first Chester-built Heron Series 2 was handed over to the French carrier Union Aeromaritime de Transportes (UAT) on 7 March 1953 and was later sold in the Congo and used by the ill-fated President Tshombe of Katanga.

Royal choice: XM296, one of the fleet of four VIP Herons chosen by HM The Queen's Flight – built and serviced for many years at Chester and based at Royal Air Force Benson, Oxfordshire – at the opening of London-Gatwick Airport by HM The Queen on 9 June 1958. The other three aircraft were: XM295, XM375 and XM391. These aircraft were flown extensively by HRH Prince Philip. They also made numerous overseas tours between 1958 and 1963 with the British Royal Family, numerous overseas monarchs and presidents, and home and overseas political leaders. They flew a total distance of two million miles and a total flying time of 13,400 hours. Several overseas potentates also chose the Heron for their personal use.

Airline choice: Chester-built Heron 2 G-ANLN serving with Jersey Airlines as Duchess of Guernsey, illustrating the commercial popularity of the Heron. This aircraft, one of two in the fleet (together with three ex-West African Airways aircraft), later converted (at DH Leavesden) for military communications under the designation Sea Heron C.Mk.1 XR441 to serve with 781 Squadron Royal Navy at Lee-on-Solent. In May 1961 the Royal Navy decided to replace five Sea Devons (the naval version of the Dove) with a similar number of ex-civil Heron 2s.

Business choice: Chester-built Heron 2 G-AOGW Golf Whiskey used for many years as part of the company transport aircraft fleet of Vickers-Armstrongs (Aircraft) at Weybridge, Surrey, and based at the nearby flight test airfield at Wisley. The Heron proved to be an ideal choice as a corporate communications aircraft and was a logical progression from the Dove. Chester-built Herons were notably used by Rolls-Royce, English Electric, Ferranti, British Aircraft Corporation (BAC) and the Royal Aircraft Establishment (RAE) in the UK; and overseas by Phillips of the Netherlands and Fiat of Italy.

Military choice: Chester-built Royal Navy Heron C.Mk.4 XR391 serving with 781 Squadron. Military Herons, with their 'four-engine safety' attribute, were also supplied from Chester to the RAF and the communications flights of the air forces of Saudi Arabia, South Africa, Ceylon, Iraq, West Germany, Jordan and Ghana. These included one once maintained as the personal aircraft of King Feisal of Iraq, and those frequently used by King Hussein of Jordan and President Nkrumah Of Ghana.

*The first Chester-built DH106 Comet 2 fuselage, with the original rectangular-shaped passenger windows, nearing completion in midst of large-scale production of Vampire Trainer cockpit/nose fuselage sections (with a Chipmunk, lower left).*

*Comet 2 fuselages, together with other airframe components and tooling, being shipped by barge to Chester via Liverpool docks. It was en route from the moribund second Comet assembly line started by Short Brothers at Belfast but abandoned when all Comet production was halted after the early in-service Comet accidents. A number of other Royal Air Force production contracts were directed to Northern Ireland, e.g., the Bristol Britannia, Vickers-Supermarine Swift (not activated) and a front fuselage section of the Vickers VC10.*

*The Belfast-built Comet 2 fuselage being towed past the Tudor-faced architecture of the historic Roman-walled city of Chester and thus honouring the name by which the Broughton Aircraft Factory and Hawarden Aerodrome complex became known over much of its history.*

*Despite the suspension of the initial Chester Comet 2 line in 1954, reworked Comet 1A and 2 airframes for the RAF and others were completed at Chester between 1955 and 1957 and served as an educational operation for the building of the strengthened and enlarged Comet 4. Scaffolding was used for access to these much bigger aircraft untill the construction of two-deck staging. Production of the diminutive Vampire, Venom, Dove and Heron was to continue throughout the next decade alongside the radically different manufacturing scale and techniques of the Comet.*

The second of two Comet 1A VIP transports, VC5302, built at Hatfield for the Royal Canadian Air Force Air Transport Command in 1953, being re-accepted outside the Chester flight shed on 26 September 1957 after major fuselage strengthening and conversion to Comet 1XB standard. Used by HM The Queen and Prince Philip during their visit to Canada in 1959, this aircraft remained in service until October 1964. The last of the original Comet 1s, these two aircraft were used to simulate high-speed jet bomber penetration to test the Canadian defences. The first built was also the first jet transport to cross the Atlantic when delivered to No.412 squadron at Rockcliffe, Ontario, on 29 May 1953. Two Hatfield-built Comet 1As, acquired by the UK Ministry of Supply in 1954, were similarly modified at Chester in 1958 for experimental use by the Royal Aircraft Establishment (RAE).

The Royal Air Force Comet 2R XK663, originally intended for commercial operation with British Overseas Airways Corporation (BOAC). It was one of fifteen Hatfield-built Comet 2s later converted at Chester to 2.R and T.2 standards for the RAF, for transport and training roles, and delivered to No.192 and No.216 Squadrons respectively between 1956 and 1958. These aircraft were complemented by the only Chester-built RAF Comet 2 XK716, named 'Cepheus', and delivered to No.216 Squadron in May 1957 – which became the world's first military jet transport squadron. The RAF Comet 2 was also the world's first 'stretched' jet airliner. The XK716 was the only Comet built from assemblies produced by Shorts of Belfast, and also the last Comet 2 before both Hatfield and Chester began production of the enlarged Comet 4. Twenty-five Comet 2s were to have been built at Chester but the BOAC in-service disasters led to them all being cancelled, although four had been partially completed.

The first Chester-built Comet 4 fuselages – notably incorporating oval passenger window cut-outs instead of the rectangular-shaped ones of the original Comet design – nearing the proof-pressure testing stage in early 1958. The Chester Factory also became responsible for the manufacture of a number of large sub-assemblies for the Hatfield Comet 4 production line.

The original factory-wide overhead crane system at the Chester Factory adapted to lift and greatly simplify the mating of the complete Comet 4 fuselage and wing structures (here for the second East African Airways aircraft). This demonstrates the well-matched scale of the Chester assembly area to that of the largest aircraft type to be built at Chester. The crane drivers (who were invariably female) quickly became adept at swinging these very large loads with ease for precise positioning.

*The G-APDE, the first Chester-built Comet 4 for BOAC, and the fourth of the airline's order of twenty, being made ready for its first flight. It was taken from the Hawarden Aerodrome, on 20 September 1958, to Hatfield for flight testing, customer acceptance and delivery on 2 October – two days before two Hatfield-built BOAC Comet 4s inaugurated the historic world's first transatlantic jet airliner service between London and New York. G-APDE notably operated the first jet service between London and Singapore.*

*G-APDR, the seventh Chester-built Comet 4 for BOAC leaving the flight shed for its first flight on 9 July 1959 and delivery 11 days later on 20 July 1959. Five more BOAC aircraft were delivered by the end of that year. Altogether, twelve Comets 4s were built at Chester for BOAC, the last being G-APDJ delivered on 11 January 1960, two months ahead of schedule. Together with the single Chester-built Comet C2 for the Royal Air Force, this brought the total Chester Comet output to thirteen before the de Havilland Aircraft Co. became part of the Hawker Siddeley Group in January 1960. However, all subsequent Comets built at both Hatfield and Chester continued to carry the DH prefix with the final delivery on 26 February 1964.*

## Six

# Under the Hawker Siddeley Banner

Although the Government-directed consolidation of the UK aircraft industry in January 1960 resulted in the pioneering de Havilland company being subsumed into the Hawker Siddeley Group (HSG), the DH name was to prevail for a further 4½ years as the HS de Havilland Division until the firm became fully absorbed into Hawker Siddeley Aviation (HSA) in June 1965.

During the 17 years of operation under the Hawker Siddeley banner, the Chester Factory saw the final stages of the production of the DH Vampire Trainer (8), Dove (35) and Heron (11); and the production of the Comet 4 (28), Sea Vixen (30) and DH Canada Beaver (46). However, the three great sustainers at Chester were the successful DH/HS 125 business jet, the main airframe components for the Comet-based HS801 Nimrod maritime patrol aircraft (41), and the private contract supply of wing structures for the European Airbus airliner consortium. Completing the first wing set in November 1971, the Government-directed formation of British Aerospace (BAe) in April 1977 meant that HSA bequeathed the new company this increasingly successful aerostructures programme and continuing high-volume output of the 125 and, most importantly, the exceptional capability and record of the Chester site.

*The facade of the original management and administration block fronting the main Chester Factory and up-dated for the third time in mid-1963 to incorporate the Hawker Siddeley Aviation Limited title. Its previous incarnations were: the Hawker Siddeley Group, in place from 1960 to 1963, de Havilland Aircraft Company from mid-1948, and the founding Vickers-Armstrongs Limited from 1939.*

*Right foreground: forward section of the Comet 4 fuselage panel manufacture (situated immediately behind the flight deck, assembled separately). The third section is that for the over-wing fuselage component and incorporates the large over-wing emergency escape hatches, as well as the redesigned oval passenger window apertures.*

*Civil Comet 4 final assembly in full swing on two assembly lines in the early 1960s with the first of a fleet of nine Comet 4Cs for Misrair/United Arab Airlines, the national flag carrier of Egypt, at the livery application stage. Built between May 1960 and February 1964, this airline's Comet fleet was flown extensively throughout the Middle East, the Mediterranean, Europe and North Africa. Other civil Comet 4s built at Chester under the Hawker Siddeley banner between July 1960 and February 1964 included: three each for East African Airways and Aerolineas Argentinas; three (longer-bodied) 4Cs for Middle East Airlines; two short-haul (also longer-bodied) 4Bs for British European Airways; and two 4Cs for Kuwait Airways.*

Military Comet C.4 production for Royal Air Force Transport Command, built to serve with No.216 Squadron. In 1975 all were acquired by the UK independent airline, Dan-Air of London, to become the last of a total fleet of forty-eight pre-owned Comet 4s of all types (including some for spares) which enabled the airline to become the largest Comet operator.

Royal Air Force Comet C.4 XR395, the first of the five such aircraft – which in civil guise became G-BDIT. XR398. the fourth became G-BDIW and made the final Comet commercial flight on 9 November 1980, before retirement in February 1981 for preservation at Dusseldorf, Germany. Other ex-Dan-Air Comets have notably survived at Duxford, Cambridgeshire (G-APDA); Wroughton, Wiltshire (G-APYD); and East Fortune, Lothian, Scotland (G-BDIX). Dan-Air Comet 4s carried more than eight million passengers between 1966 and 1980.

Chester-built Comet 4C XS235 which was the last Comet flying, up to 14 March 1997, before being acquired by de Havilland Heritage. Here it is saluting its original home at Broughton while being ferried to Bruntingthorpe, Leicestershire, on 30 October 1997, to be maintained by the British Aviation Heritage Group, with the hope that it will eventually be made airworthy again. On its first flight to Hatfield on 26 September 1963 to be fitted out as a flying radio and avionics laboratory, it was named Canopus. During its 30 years in service, it served with the Blind Landing Experimental Unit (BLEU), Bedford; the Aircraft and Armament Experimental Establishment (A&AEE) at Boscombe Down; and the Defence Test Evaluation Organisation (DETO) at Farnborough.

Centre: John Cunningham, the famous DH Chief Test Pilot with, left: his deputy, Pat Fillingham and, right: E. 'Bracks' Brackstone Browne, Chief Flight Test Engineer, with the penultimate production Comet at Chester. Originally a Comet 4C, built 'on spec' without a committed customer, it was first flown (registered G-5-1) on 25 October 1965. After storage, this aircraft was reactivated with the military serial XV147 and flown to HSA Woodford (Manchester) to become the aerodynamic development prototype for the HS801 Nimrod maritime patrol aircraft (but retaining its Rolls-Royce Avon engines) and first flown there in this guise on 31 July 1967. (In 1953, Fillingham had flown a DH Chipmunk to victory in the King's Cup Air Race averaging 140mph.)

De Havilland Canada DHC.2 Beaver AL Mk.1 XP770 high-wing STOL, 'half-ton-truck' bush transport aircraft, one of the original order for thiry-six of these aircraft assembled at HSA Chester in 1961 and 1962 for the British Army Air Corps, plus four for the Ministry of Defence, awaiting delivery on the ramp outside the flight shed. Although adequately equipped for reconnaissance, the British Army Air Corps required the Beaver for liaison duties and casualty evacuation in conditions of field support where the availability of prepared surfaces could not be counted on. A supplementary order for a further six Army aircraft was completed in 1962. The four aircraft ex-MoD with RAF serials XR213-216 were alloted to the Muscat and Oman Air Force.

Air-testing of DHC.2 Beaver XP769, one of the forty-six Chester-assembled Beaver light military transport aircraft built from kits of the main components manufactured by the Canadian de Havilland plant at Downsview, Toronto, which were shipped to Chester where British equipment including radio and instruments were fitted. Although one example of the type, G-ANAR, was experimentally converted by DH Canada with the British-made Alvis Leonides engine, a revised tail unit and extended wings, all the Chester-assembled Beavers retained the original standard Pratt and Whitney Wasp Junior engine.

XP918, the first of thirty DH 110 Sea Vixen aircraft built at Chester for the Royal Navy when the last phase of production of this aircraft type was transferred from the DH Christchurch, Dorset, Factory in 1962. After this, the last FAW Mk.1, there were twenty-nine aircraft of the FAW Mk.2 version built during the ensuing four years, incorporating overall improvements to the weapon system, together with increased fuel tank volume in forward over-wing extensions of the twin-boom structures – the last flew on 3 February 1966. A further thirty-seven Christchurch-built Mk.1s were also converted at Chester to the Mk.2 standard between 1965 and 1968. The first of these, XJ580, was the last Sea Vixen to fly in RN colours and, after a 20-year service life, has now been donated to the Tangmere Military Aviation Museum by the Sea Vixen Society.

Originally designed and built by de Havilland at Hatfield as a jet replacement for the Dove and Heron, the DH125 500mph business jet was first flown there as a prototype on 13 August 1962. After the second aircraft, full-scale production was transferred to Chester to enable the Hatfield team to concentrate on the Trident airliner (first flown on 9 January 1962 but the only DH type for which Chester was not primarily involved). The first Chester-built DH125, G-ARYC, flew on 16 February 1963 and by mid-1964, components for the fourteenth (now re-designated) HS125 aircraft were entering final assembly, initial release to production of sixty aircraft was implemented, and transatlantic air deliveries began in July. (The folding-wing Sea Vixen naval fighter and the Comet airliner were also in continuing production at this time.)

Chester-built Sea Vixen FAW Mk.2 XP924, the sixth of the twenty-nine, first flown there in August 1963. Having served exclusively with 889 Sqn. Fleet Arm on the carrier HMS Eagle in the 1960s, this is the only remaining airworthy Sea Vixen. After restoration by de Havilland Aviation Ltd of South Wales, with the civil registration G-CVIX for display purposes from 2001, it has been based at Hurn (Bournemouth). Flying in the colours of the Red Bull drinks manufacturer since 2003, it was returned in 2007 to the original 899 Sqn. colours and registration that it carried before its retirement from the frontline in 1971. The Sea Vixen was the third and largest development of the distinctive DH twin-boom jet fighter concept and the heaviest aircraft to enter British naval service. It was the first British interceptor to dispense with guns, Britain's first naval aircraft design as an integrated weapons system, and the first to become operational armed with guided weapons. In the all-weather role, it was equipped with DH Firestreak air-to-air infra-red homing missiles and retractable rocket pods.

The 100th HS125 business jet, a Series 1A for the US market (but with the 'DH' prefix retained because of the de Havilland name being much better-known and preferred there), leaving the Chester production line on 15 July 1966, and at which time production output was already seven aircraft a month. As the archetypal business jet, and increasingly the mainstay of the Chester output with well over 1,000 people now involved in the programme, many aircraft were being built and flown as 'green' (unfurnished) airframes – as typified by this one. Interior furnishings and custom equipment were installed by one of Hawker Siddeley's three North American distributors engaged in late 1963, Atlantic Sales Corporation of Wilmington, Delaware (the other two being AiResearch Aviation Services of Los Angeles and Timmins Aviation of Montreal, Canada). This event set a precedent for the celebration of several centennial deliveries thereafter.

An HS125 Series 3B G-AWMS built in 1969 for the RTZ (Rio Tinto Zinc) mining company at the pre-delivery flight test stage outside the former fire station and flight test offices fronting the flight shed. This model exemplified an early stage of continuous all-round development of the breed, in particular with new engines and avionic equipment, that has characterised the 125 programme from the outset of its production life to meet the needs of its diverse global appeal.

In December 1969, Hawker Siddeley joined forces with Beech Aircraft Corporation of Wichita, Kansas, as distributors of all 125s in North America and in which market the aircraft was renamed the Beechcraft Hawker BH125. Beech also agreed to purchase forty green aircraft from the Chester line and complete them as BH125s to customer requirements. This partnership was eventually severed in September 1975 when Hawker Siddeley Aviation Inc. was formed to handle HS125 sales in the USA and Mexico. (Nineteen years later, the partnership was effectively reinstated when, in 1993, Raytheon Aircraft Company, which had acquired Beech in the meantime, bought the British Aerospace Corporate Jets Co. but continued to source 125 airframes from Chester under production licence).

An HS125 Series 400A green 'airframe' destined for an unnamed American customer, but already carrying an American registration, N57BH, being readied outside the Chester flight shed in May 1971 for delivery to become a BH125. North Atlantic delivery flights were made via Iceland, Greenland and Goose Bay, Labrador (Canada). This was the route that had been pioneered by the RAF with a six-aircraft DH Vampire F.3 flight in July 1948 (the first jet aircraft to cross the Atlantic under their own power). It was also used extensively by Vickers-Armstrongs from the mid-1950s for deliveries of the Viscount to North American customers.

Six of the eventual fleet of twenty HS125 Series 2s produced at Chester during the 1960s for the Royal Air Force as Dominie T.Mk.1 air navigation trainers awaiting delivery, initially to No.1 Air Navigation School at Stradishall, Suffolk. The RAF Dominie fleet is today located at the RAF College at Cranwell, Lincolnshire. The name was a Scottish term for schoolmaster and had originally been used by de Havilland for the pre-war DH89 Dragon Rapide twin-engined biplane when deployed by the RAF as a navigation trainer during the Second World War. When on 31 March 1995, 32 Squadron – the former Metropolitan Communications Squadron – amalgamated with The Queen's Flight and marking the end of dedicated royal flying in the RAF, the 'new' unit designated 32 (TR) The Royal Squadron, deployed the six inherited 125 CC.3s, in service since 1982 until 2011, in transporting government ministers, VIPs and high-ranking military personnel, as well as royalty. At least one aircraft was always deployed in Bahrain in connection with the UK's military involvement in Iraq and Afghanistan, while another was usually with Hawker Beechcraft at Broughton for modifications and upgrades. Many other 125s were subsequently to issue from the Chester line for military applications, civil aviation pilot training and airways calibration duties.

XV148, the second and fully representative HS801 Nimrod development prototype, in final assembly at Chester. The British Government had announced the conception of the Nimrod ('The Mighty Hunter') on 2 February 1965 as the world's first (and still the only) land-based pure jet long-range maritime reconnaissance, anti-submarine and search-and-rescue aircraft. It was based on the well-proven Comet 4 airframe, and to replace the venerable Avro Shackleton (of which a large number had been overhauled at Chester in the early 1960s).

XR148 being made ready for its maiden flight at Hawarden on 23 May 1967. Initially completed at Chester in mid-1965 as the second of two unsold civil Comet 4Cs, and stored without being flown, this aircraft was then converted there for the Ministry of Defence, complete with the navigation and attack systems, and Rolls-Royce Spey engines in place of the original Avons.

*XV814, the ex-BOAC (DH Hatfield-built) Comet 4 G-APDF which was sold to the Ministry of Technology and converted at Chester before being delivered to the Royal Aircraft Establishment (RAE), Farnborough, in October 1968. There they used it as a spacious long-range platform for military communications equipment development. Later acquiring a Nimrod fin and rudder from the first prototype, XV147, this aircraft inevitably acquired the soubriquet 'Comrod'*

Several Chester-built Comet 4s were used in the complex Nimrod development programme. In 1977, the Chester-built ex-BOAC Comet 4 G-APDS became XW626, the development aircraft for the bulbous nose-mounted GEC radar for the (later abandoned) Airborne Early Warning Nimrod AEW Mk.3.

*Main fuselage production line for the original HS801 Nimrod Mk.1 at Chester in the late 1960s (alongside continuing high-rate production of the HS125 business jet). The two Chester-built Nimrod development prototypes, XV147 and XV148, were the precursors of all forty-one original Nimrod production aircraft fuselages, wings and other components at Chester between 1966 and 1970 (38 MR.1 maritime reconnaissance and three R.1 electronic surveillance). These major airframe components were then driven to HSA Woodford for the addition of the 'bath-tub bubble' skirt structure of the unpressurised weapons bay onto the underside of the slender Comet airliner antecedent and for final assembly, equipping and delivery.*

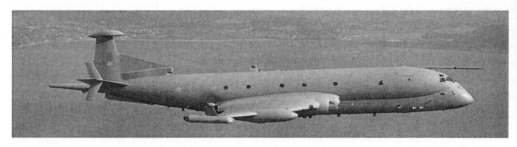

*Nimrod MRA4 ZJ518, one of the 12 ex-HSA 801 Nimrod MR.2 maritime patrol and reconnaissance aircraft after being converted, at what had become BAE Systems Woodford, to the new-generation Nimrod MRA.4 standard with new wings, lower fuselage, tail sections, engines, flightdeck, fuselage interior and mission systems to provide a greatly enhanced capability. These aircraft had already been converted from Mk.1 and Mk.2 standard at Woodford between 1975 and 1984. However, after the Nimrod MR.2 fleet had been withdrawn from service on 31 March 2010 the protracted MRA.4 progamme was peremptorily cancelled in the UK Government's Strategic Defence and Security Review (SDSR) of October 2010. (The remaining two Nimrod R.1s were finally stood down on 30 June 2011). Nevertheless, it is significant that the original Chester-built Nimrod fuselage of the late 1960s was the only major airframe component retained in this intended major up-grade, having been found to be in continuing excellent condition after two successive strip-downs – thus constituting an outstanding tribute to the original Chester workmanship. Consequently, the 42 years of sterling Nimrod operational service since 1969 – with RAF 43(R), 51, 120, 210 and 206 squadrons – extended the total life of the DH Comet genus and ancestry, in which the Chester factory had played such a leading role, to nearly six decades. MR.2 XV244 and the nose and forward fuselage of MR.2 XV240 have been acquired for the proposed Morayavia Aerospace Centre in the Kinloss, Scotland, area. The last two ex-51 Squadron R.1s XW664 and XW249, are being preserved at the Aeropark at East Midlands Airport, near Nottingham, and the RAF Museum at Cosford, Shropshire, respectively; and the nose and forward fuselage of R.1 XW665 is preserved at the Technik Museum Speyer, near Heidelberg, Germany.*

---

### HERITAGE AND ADVENTURER PROJECTS

Like many other British aircraft manufacturing sites, in the de Havilland and Hawker Siddeley years, the Chester/Broughton Aircraft Repair and Overhaul Organisation (AROO), also undertook several company-related heritage restoration and adventurer projects, together with retirees and other volunteers, notably including:

- Maintenance and support of the company-owned DH98 Mosquito T.III RR299 (G-ASKH) noted on p. 84.

- Preparation and support of the DH89 Rapide G-AIYR for David and Cherry Cyster's flight to South Africa and back in 1980 to commemorate Alan Cobham's 1925 flight.

- Preparation and support of the DH80 Puss Moth G-AAZP for R.P. Williams and H. Labouchere's flight to Australia in 1984.

- The rebuild of the 1924 vintage DH51 G-EBIR (VP-KAA 'Miss Kenya') for the Shuttleworth Trust at Old Warden, Bedfordshire, completed in March 1973 and test flown by famous DH/HS test pilots, John Cunningham and Pat Fillingham, before delivery.

- Restoration of the 1936 vintage DH87b 'Hornet Moth' G-ADND completed in early 1976.

- Maintenance of the Sport's Club's aircraft – originally two Tiger Moths and Puss Moth G-AAZP; later two Chipmunks and a Tiger Moth.

*Foreground: one of the two HS748s that were transferred from Woodford to Chester for final assembly in December 1974, at the peak of Nimrod work there, and were then delivered to Germany.*

*Fuselages of the first four of 12 ex-HSA 801 Nimrod MR2 maritime patrol and reconnaissance aircraft in the final assembly area at what is today BAE Systems Woodford (Manchester) – for the second time for the major up-grade to the new generation BAE Systems Nimrod MRA4 maritime reconnaissance and attack standard there. Significantly, the original Chester-built Nimrod fuselage structure of the late 1960s is the only major airframe component being retained in this major up-grade, having been found to be in continuing excellent condition on strip-down. These aircraft had already been converted from Mk.1 to Mk.2 standard at HSA/BAe Woodford between 1975 and 1984 and serving with 43(R), 120, 210 and 206 squadrons based at Kinloss, Morayshire, Scotland.*

The sculpture machining of rolled and forged aluminium billets to form the skin cover panels for the wing structural box/fuel tank of the Airbus A300 – the worlds' first wide-body, twin-aisle, twin-jet airliner. This was done on custom-built, numerically controlled, long-bed (60ft x 12ft air cushion/vacuum suction bed) machine tools installed in what had been the main aircraft assembly hall of the Chester Factory. In 1969, Hawker Siddeley had courageously elected to become a private contract partner in the European Airbus Industrie (AI) airliner programme consortium (formally constituted in December 1970) to supply wing structures designed at Hatfield and manufactured at Chester. This had required considerable new investment in what were the largest high-speed profile-milling and routing machines in Europe, made by Marwin of Leicester and Cramic of Southall, Middlesex, to produce these 50ft-long wing skin panels. A 1,200-ton hydraulic horizontal-acting press was also acquired from Shaw of Salford, Lancashire, for pre-forming the access door-perforated underside panels.

Sculpture-machined Airbus A300 inner and outer wing skin panels incorporating separately attached open L-section stiffening and stabilising stringers, fuel tank access door cut-outs and sealing compound, prior to final assembly in (four of) the six sets of upright assembly jigs in the background. By mid-1976, with orders for 100 complete wing sets, plus authorisation for a further thrty-two sets of advance materials, Chester had produced eighty wing sets, each worth more than £2 million at that time.

An American Gemcor Drivmatic, automated and numerically controlled, squeeze riveting machine of the type widely used in Airbus wing machined skin/stringer panel assembly at Chester since the 1970s and which have proved to be ideal for the heavy duty operation involved. These machines automatically drill and countersink the holes in the metal, form the rivets from metal blanks, fit and clench them, machine the heads flush with the wing skin outer surface and then move the whole structure to the precise position for insertion of the next rivet. The whole operation is monitored by CCTV cameras mounted above and below the structural assembly. American Spacematic and Quackenbush drill motor equipment was adopted early for the great proliferation of skin-to-structure bolt fastenings applied during the in-jig assembly operation.

The removal from the assembly jig at Chester of the first (port) Airbus A300 airliner two-part wing structure on 11 August 1971 – the first significant Chester contribution to this new pan-European commercial aircraft industrial mosaic. Moved in a specially designed lifting cradle, supported by the overhead crane rail system, this structure was an almost totally machined and integrally sealed 'wet' wing torsion box/fuel tank construction. This airliner wing manufacturing technique had already been well established in the UK by Hawker Siddeley, Vickers-Armstrongs and British Aircraft Corporation.

Out-of-jig completion of Airbus A300 wing structures with the attachment of secondary structural items prior to aerial transport first to VFW Bremen, for equipping and then to the Airbus Industrie final assembly centre at Aerospatiale, Toulouse. Initially, the completed structures were moved up to a specially designed British Cramic machine to trim-finish the root profile to match the joint attachments on the wing/fuselage centre section, top right, but this later became unnecessary. The detail design and parts supply chain for these huge structures engaged six HSA factories, co-ordinated from the parent plant at Hatfield: Chester, Hatfield, Woodford and Chadderton (near Manchester), Brough (Yorkshire) and Hamble (near Southampton).

Out-of-jig completion of Airbus A300 and A310 wing structures in the early 1980s. Top right corner: note the contrasting scale of these wings with that of the diminutive HS125 complete airframe in continuous parallel production.

# Seven

# British Aerospace and Airbus Wings the World Over

The creation of British Aerospace (BAe) in April 1977 resulted in the Hawker Siddeley Aviation Hatfield-Chester Division becoming the similarly named division of the BAe Aircraft Group from 1 January 1978. BAe joined Airbus Industrie as a full 20 per cent equity-holding partner on 1 January 1979. The expansion of Airbus wing manufacture and continuing production of the 125 business jet were the twin staples of the Chester Factory output during the ensuing twenty-two year BAe era. The closure of the long-established Hatfield parent plant in Autumn 1993 also resulted in Chester becoming conjoined with Filton (Bristol) as the divisional management and design centre of the Airbus Division of British Aerospace (Commercial Aircraft) Limited in 1989. It continued as the exclusive wing manufacturing centre for every member of the growing Airbus airliner dynasty; as well as the enduring 125 (with airframe component kits for Raytheon of the USA after it acquired BAe Corporate Jets in January 1993). The factory completed the 2,000th Airbus wing set in early 1999 and became known exclusively as 'Broughton', a geographically correct name in deference to Welsh devolution. Major new extensions and equipping for the newest Airbus derivatives were also begun during 1999, preceding the formation of BAE Systems on 30 November 1999.

*When British Aerospace (Commercial Aircraft) Ltd was formed on 1 January 1989, the newly clad wing despatch building was the ideal location to proclaim the Airbus Division formed a month later. It was the loading and aerial delivery point for the finished product and the aerial arrival point of visitors and customers to the Chester site. The BAe Corporate Aircraft Division was also established at this time to handle continuing manufacturing and sales of the (now further re-designated) BAe125.*

These fourteen aircraft at Chester on 23 May 1985 typify the celebrations of centennial production and/or sales events in the prolific and enduring Hawker Siddeley/British Aerospace 125 business jet programme. This event united almost every version of the aircraft with the celebration of the sale of the 600th example into a market which by then embraced thirty-seven countries worldwide with 60 per cent of the output exported to North America. The latest version, the Series 800 in the foreground, notably offered a 3,000 nautical mile intercontinental-range and an Electronic Flight Instrument System (EFIS) equipped flight deck (the 100th sale of this version was announced on 24 October 1987). Total BAe 125 800 sales were 319 aircraft (following 576 Series 1 to 700).

The first BAe 125 Series 1000 corporate jet – registered G-EXLR, standing for EXtended Long Range (and 'Elixir' for the corresponding market invigoration) – making its first 'ceremonial first flight' at Chester on 28 June 1990 (it had made its actual first flight there on 16 June). This aircraft was then transferred to the BAe civil flight test centre at Woodford (Manchester). This was the last BAe development of the type and all 125 production under the BAe aegis at Chester ceased in 1996 – 33 years after first flight of the first Chester-built 125 in February 1963 – with the completion of 42 Series 1000s and a grand total of 869 of the 125 genus before BAe sold its Corporate Jets business to Raytheon of the USA. Since continuing to build 125 primary airframe components under sub-contract to Raytheon for final assembly and marketing by that company at Wichita, Kansas, USA, the Chester/Broughton site was involved in the 125 programme for an incredible 50 years before its cessation in 2012 – after a grand total of 1,725 complete fly-way aircraft and airframe kits had been built there.

*Celebrating the emergence of the first wing box structure for the Airbus single-aisle A320 from the assembly jig on 3 October 1985 – three weeks ahead of schedule. Both wing boxes then left Chester by road on 28 November – prominently labelled as such and placarded 'Beware of Fast Mover' – for transport to the BAe Airbus Division Filton (Bristol) site, arriving there the same day, for equipping prior to despatch to Toulouse for final assembly.*

*Equipping the Airbus A320 family (A320/A321/A319/A318) wings at Broughton with secondary and wing-tip fixed structures, leading- and trailing-edge flying control surfaces and fuel and de-icing systems on the Single-Aisle Wing (SAW) flow-line facility, which became fully operational in February 2002 as part of the factory-wide lean manufacturing programme.*

A completed 98ft/30m wing torsion box structure for the Airbus A340 after removal from the multi-level assembly jig – by an inflatable air-bag 'hovercraft-style' raft. After initially being transported in pairs by Super Guppy aircraft to Bremen for equipping, they are flown on to Toulouse singly for final assembly because of the consequent extended dimensions in relation to those of the upper fuselage cross-section of both the Super Guppy and the succeeding Super Transporter aircraft. The A340 was the first four-jet long-range derivative of the Airbus family, with a range of up to 15,000km, and has been flying in scheduled service with Chester-made wings since 1993.

The 1,500th set of Airbus wings being loaded into an Airbus Super Transporter aircraft at the BAe Chester Factory in August 1996, destined for the German Airbus assembly centre at Hamburg. This wing set was for an A319 – the smallest Airbus type at that time – and appropriately part of an order for the German airline Lufthansa. At that time, BAe stated that 300 other companies and 25,000 workers in Britain were involved in Airbus design and manufacture and that throughout the UK Airbus business accounted for nearly 1.5 per cent of total national manufacturing exports and was contributing £1 billion to the annual trade balance.

The new 100ft long wing skin panel milling machine made by MPS of Leicester for the extended span Airbus A340-500/600 series, installed during 1999, the largest and longest to date. Those installed at Chester in the early 1970s to produce the 50ft-long panels for the two-part Airbus A300 wing were the largest in Europe, until in 1984 the world's largest routing machine was brought into operation, the machine bed measuring 66m x 3.75m and weighing 532 tonnes. The cutting heads of the KTM 200 machines that were installed in 1990 were also fully overhauled and up-dated by Giddings and Lewis of Southampton in 1999.

The new vertical wing spar milling machine built by Ingersoll of Rockford, Illinois, USA, with vertical part holding, linear motors and large flood coolant tanks, installed in 1999. The Broughton wing skin and spar machine shop was complemented by a major new anodising process treatment and painting facility also commissioned during 1999. Fully automated, the twelve-tank facility includes a washing, degreasing and rinsing line to cleanse incoming components, followed by deoxidisation and chromic acid processes, before air-drying and painting. With computer-controlled cranes, each with a maximum capacity of four tonnes to manoeuvre components through the process line, this huge facility can process thirty-four flight bar loads per day.

Two of four large-scale 'state of the art' electro-impact Low Voltage Electromagnetic Riveter (LVER) machines installed in 1999 to enhance the capability of automated panel assembly with precision drilling and insertion of the many large-size bolt and rivet fasteners which attach the machined strengthening stringers to the wing panels. Modelled on the Airbus A320 wing skin LVER riveter, these machines incorporated faster insertion speeds and a 'cold-working' facility into the process. Each set of single-aisle aircraft wings, the smallest produced, requires around 10,000 rivets and 16,000 bolts.

# Eight

# Raytheon and Hawker Beechcraft Corporate Jets

The acquisition of British Aerospace's 125 corporate jets business by Raytheon of the USA on 1 June 1993, together with the 'Hawker' marketing prefix from the Hawker Siddeley company, was also accompanied by a sub-contract manufacturing agreement with BAe for airframe component kits to continue to be made at Broughton before being shipped for final assembly of the aircraft at Raytheon's Wichita, Kansas, plant. An up-graded version of the BAe 125-800 was renamed the Hawker 800XP (extra performance). Now 14 years on, these airframe components continue to be made at Broughton – but in a separate and discrete area of the factory from the primary Airbus wing manufacturing work. In 1994, Raytheon also became established on the Broughton site in its own right in the former BAe125 twin-hangar service centre, operating a 125/Hawker service centre as Raytheon Aircraft Services Ltd (RASL). In 1998, Raytheon began extending its capabilities at the centre to include specialised conversions before consolidating this work in one hangar, and in 2002 establishing Raytheon Systems Ltd (RSL) in the other hangar as the prime contractor for the development of the air and ground segments of the ASTOR (Airborne Stand-Off Radar) system for the UK Ministry of Defence (MoD). Consequently, Broughton is also benefiting from technology transfer from the USA. At the beginning of 2007, Raytheon sold its commercial aircraft business to a new private equity company which re-named it Hawker Beechcraft. The twin-hangar complex was then acquired by Marshall Aviation Services in August 2013.

Previous page: *The twin-hangar (originally RAF MU K-type) now Hawker Beechcraft (left) and Raytheon Systems (right) stand-alone, management and operational facility to the north-east of the Broughton site is leased from, and shared with, Airbus UK. Since 1994, the former company has operated a fully approved service centre for Raytheon's 'Hawkers' and other similar business jets operating in Europe, Africa and the Middle East, and which in 1997 was fully integrated into the company's global network. Specializing in maintenance and modification of this class of aircraft, its capabilities include design, avionics repair, interior custom adaptation, refurbishment and upholstery, engine overhaul and parts manufacture approval. The company also has a multi-discipline supply management team which manages the sub-tier supplier base for the Hawker aircraft now assembled in the USA. The Raytheon Systems unit is a first-tier supplier to the MoD as prime contractor for the ASTOR programme.*

*The interior of the Raytheon Systems hangar with three of the five-strong fleet of Canadian Bombardier Global Express baseline aircraft being specially modified to form the air segment for the ASTOR programme (together with the integration of the supporting ground stations equipment). To be designated Sentinel R.Mk.1 in RAF service, these aircraft will provide vastly expanded reconnaissance, surveillance and situational awareness capabilities extending into command and control, intelligence-gathering and communications across the huge areas of future battle-space and replace the recently retired venerable English Electric Canberra PR9.*

*Sentinel ZJ692 departing from Broughton on 16 March 2006, bound for Greenville, Texas, USA, for development and evaluation flying. The first aircraft, ZJ690, was formally handed over to No.5 Squadron RAF at Waddington, Lincolnshire, on 6 June 2007, and initial operational capability will be established in 2008, the full five-aircraft fleet operational capability was achieved in 2009, thus providing the British armed services with a transformational network-centric air (and ground-integrated) reconnaissance system that is claimed to be far ahead of any other similar system anywhere in the world.*

# Nine

# BAe Systems and Airbus UK into the New Millennium

Broughton (now the exclusive site name) entered the new millennium under the banner of the newly formed BAE Systems – which was created on 30 November 1999 by the merger of the former British Aerospace (BAe) and GEC-Marconi Electronic Systems (MES). Broughton then became part of Airbus UK Ltd, formed by BAE Systems on 30 March 2000 in anticipation of the announcement of the long gestated pan-european Airbus Integrated Company (AIC), which came on 23 June 2000. The new autonomous Airbus company became operational from 1 January 2001, fully constituted on 15 July 2001, and within which Broughton continues to operate integrally with the Airbus UK management, design and manufacturing centre at Filton (Bristol). Spurred by the courage and value of the vindicated Hawker Siddeley decision to become a private venture partner to the fledgling Airbus consortium nearly 40 years ago, and massively developed through the twenty-two-year British Aerospace regime, Broughton is universally acclaimed as one of the world's most efficient and productive aerostructure producers. With well over £100 million of fresh investment in design and manufacturing facilities in 1999, Broughton entered the twenty-first century with the huge prospect and challenge of building the wings for the exciting new Airbus A380 programme that was formally launched on 9 December 2000. This most healthy business situation provided a fitting Diamond Jubilee tribute to the great heritage, capability and reputation – founded by its forebears 60 years earlier with the nation-saving Vickers Wellington – that Broughton had bequeathed to the globally successful Airbus family, the thirtieth anniversary of the founding of which it also celebrated.

*The in-jig upper-platform assembly of the main wing torsion box structure of the Airbus A340-500/600 series – the largest version in the pre-A380 Airbus production range. It has integrally end mill-routed chord-wise ribs, span-wise spars, fixed leading-edge slat support brackets, machined bottom skin cover panels and separately machined and attached stringers – prior to attachment of the top skin panel/stringers. The whole wing box assembly, incorporating the outer section made at Filton, then forms a sealed integral 'wet wing' fuel tank. This general constructional concept has characterised the entire Airbus wing family to date.*

The BAE SYSTEMS Airbus UK Broughton Factory and Hawarden Airfield, August 2000. A £100 million capital investment programme in 1999 resulted in large-scale 'millennium generation' machining, forming and treatment facilities; the corresponding buildings and infrastructure were complemented by expanded wing box assembly and equipping areas. The new facilities included: a A340-500/600 wing skin milling facility and production line; four new Low Voltage Electromagnetic Riveter (LVER) machines; a new stringer manufacturing centre; a large-scale wing spar mill; in-house wing skin, spar and stringer forming plant; automated twelve-tank treatments facility; and long-range wing equipping facility. The main new buildings, downwards from upper centre right: the twin-aisle aircraft wing equipping centre (beginning with the extension at the top right corner of the administration block and main factory); the separate (transverse) single-aisle aircraft wing equipping building; and the Metal Improvement Company (MIC) building replacing the former Deeside plant. (The £5 million 'link' building between the main factory and the former flight shed was commissioned in August 1989.) All of this development provided a world-class 'centre of excellence' for long-bed machining, processes and handling for the latest 'flow-line' manufacturing techniques for wing structures for the full range of current Airbus airliners (cf. the similar view of the site in July 1947 on page 38).

The 'Longer - Larger - Farther - Faster - Higher - Quieter - Smoother' Airbus A340-600 airliner, first flown at Toulouse on 23 April 2001, and in which an ingenious wing adaptation was incorporated.

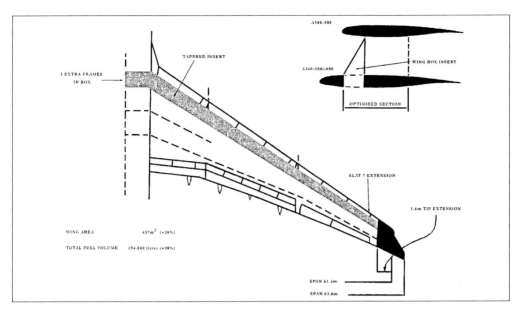

To maintain the lift and drag characteristics of the A340-500/600 long-range growth derivatives of the basic A340 design, Airbus incorporated the innovative concept of a spanwise tapered insert in the main wing structural box, rather than major wing-root 'plugs', to increase wing area and aspect ratio and re-optimise the wing section. The leading- and trailing-edge component geometrics were therefore essentially unaltered, tooling concepts were preserved, and the aerodynamic performance was close to that of an all-new wing.

The first 100ft-long A340-600 port wing, the largest and highest technology Airbus wing built at Broughton up to that time, emerging from its three-storey assembly jig in mid-April 2000 before being transferred by special lifting and inflatable air-bag pallet to the new Twin-Aisle Wing Equipping Centre, for the installation of secondary structure and fuel and other systems. It was then despatched to Bremen (singly and not as a pair as with all other Airbus type wings because its greater size and weight than the basic A340 wing) by Airbus Super Transporter aircraft for final equipping with leading- and trailing-edge control surfaces.

*Delivery loading of the first set of wings on 18 August 2001 for the diminutive 107-seat A318, the smallest member of the Airbus airliner range to be committed to production – and now also selling well as the 'Elite' in the corporate and VIP role. This is the third derivative of the highly successful 150-seat A320 'reference standard' single-aisle airliner family and complements the 125-seat (also Corporate Jet) A319 and the 185-seat A321.*

## The Broughton-Made Airbus Wing Family Millennium Parade

*Opposite*: This rising echelon 'Airbus Family Flight' was photographed at the Paris Air Show, Le Bourget, in June 1999 to celebrate the thirtieth anniversary of the launching of the initiating A300, the worlds' first twin-aisle, twin-engined jetliner, in 1969 and at the threshold of the impending new Millennium. Fortuitously, this signal event also coincided with the sixtieth anniversary of the first flight of the Broughton-made Vickers Wellington bomber in August 1939, for the large-scale production of which the plant was originally built. The formation comprises (top to bottom): the A319 Airbus Corporate Jetliner (ACJ), the A320 and A321 that then comprised the A320 single-aisle twin-jet aircraft family; the A310-300, A300-600 and A330-200 twin-jets and the four-engined A340-300 that comprise the twin-aisle long-range family; together with one of the fleet of five specially adapted A300-600T Super Transporter ('Beluga') inter-site airframe component airlifters. Taken before the arrival of the A318 and A380, the smallest and largest members respectively of the current Airbus family, this unique airliner photographic line-up is thus now also complemented by the front cover illustration of this book, all flying on Airbus UK Broughton-made wings. Together, these two formation flights effectively symbolise the high achievement of the seven-decade cavalcade of Broughton-made products and Britain's, and one of the world's, most outstanding and efficient aircraft manufacturing records. They also represent the inspiration for Broughton and all the constituent partners of the newly reconstituted Airbus organisation in its relentless pursuance of the huge airliner market prospects in the twenty-first century.

One of the more than a thousand de Havilland/Hawker Siddeley/British Aerospace Raytheon Hawker 125, and now Hawker Beechcraft, corporate business jets built at Broughton since 1962 – being fettled in the Raytheon Aircraft services centre there. The world's first jet aircraft specifically designed as a corporate communications aircraft, this diminutive world-beater has been an enduring highlight and mainstay of the prolific production output of the Broughton Factory for nearly 40 years at the turn of the Millennium and continuing strongly there in both manufacture and servicing for an incredible 50 years before its ultimate cessation in 2012, after 1,725 complete aircraft and airframe kits had been produced there. A prime export earner for Britain, the North American Dollar market has accounted for around two two thirds of total sales.

Launch impression of the new '21st Century Flagship' Airbus A380 480-650 seat double-deck airliner, the world's largest, and intended to fill the only area of the Airbus range in which the rival Boeing 747 does not have a direct competitor. In April 2000 the UK Government made available a £530 million repayable launch investment and in September 2000, the Welsh National Assembly granted a £19.5 million support package which also confirmed that the wings are to be built at Broughton. Full programme launch of the A380 (hitherto known as the A3XX) was announced on 19 December of millennium year 2000. This huge aircraft is designed within an 80m square to match existing airport aprons and taxiways and will incorporate a considerably enhanced wing and high-lift system to enable it to use existing runways.

# *Ten*

# New Giant Generation - New Factory

The sheer size and weight of the wing of the new giant generation double-deck A380, together with the ever-increasing production tempo of the overall Airbus airliner family wings in (what is now known as) the 'East Factory', meant that a wholly new A380 wing fabrication complex had to be conceived, built, equipped and commissioned in record time. Located on the opposite side of the Broughton site, and conveniently near the adjacent River Dee for the first stage of the water-borne delivery route, the resulting self-contained, purpose-built and -equipped structure is to the latest industrial standards. In this respect, particular attention has been paid to 'green' environmental considerations with the incorporation of an ingenious and highly energy-efficient 'Combined Heat and Power' (CHP) generation system. Constructed by prime contractors, Laing O'Rourke, and known as the 'West Factory', it is the largest new factory built in the UK in recent years, and employs 1,200 people. Covering a building area of 83,590 sq.m. (900,000 sq.ft) – equivalent to 12 international football pitches – and costing £350 million to build (£150 million for the building and £200 million for the machines and tooling), construction began in August 2001 and it was opened by Prime Minister, Tony Blair, on 4 July 2003. The first A380 wing box structure was delivered from the new facility on 5 April 2004. The new building will also be available for the wingbox assembly of other Airbus models when required.

September 2001: The virgin construction site with the preparatory building footprint already evident. One month later the building construction and manufacturing tooling installation area were proceeding simultaneously and the foundation area for the Electroimpact low voltage electromagnetic riveter (LVER) machines was already being located.

February 2002: Erection of the first steelwork construction above ground level. Up to this point, all work had been ground preparation and foundations, which had presented significant problems due to the high water table requiring extensive pile-driving.

Previous page: *June 2003: The completed new Broughton West Factory. Building statistics: 400m long by 200m wide, highest point 37.5m; 10,000 tonnes of primary steelwork (thirty-six times that of the operating weight empty (OWE) of the Airbus A380); 95,000 cu.m. of concrete (four times that used at the City of Manchester Stadium); 8,000 concrete piles (192km or 120 miles in length, diameters varying from 300mm to 1200mm); 50,000 cu.m of wall cladding (equivalent to six football pitches); and 52km (32 miles) of sprinkler pipework.*

# New-Generation Combined Heat and Power System

A key feature of the new West Factory is the integral installation of an environmentally innovative and highly efficient 'Combined Heat and Power System' by the British company

July 2002: Sub-assembled on the ground, and lifted into position using a 600-tonne crane, the roof structure was now receiving the cladding and there were 600 construction workers on site. With the machine tool foundation and mounting rails also complete, the LVER machines were being installed underneath the roof structure. This operation had to be screened off from the overhead and surrounding production work to avoid dust and contamination interfering with the precision positioning and measurement of this complex machinery. The 'tent' to facilitate this operation cost £1½ million.

December 2002: Although still a construction site, and under building and construction regulations, manufacture of the first wing skin/stringer panels was started on 12 December using the new LVER machines and the interior operation was already very much that of an aircraft factory. Nevertheless, this did mean that all Airbus employees had to wear industrial protective helmets and visual coats. The screening of the production area underneath the developing building also had to ensure compliance with the relevant European Joint Aviation Authority (JAA) regulations and specifications to ensure that the productive integrity was not at risk.

Aercogen, integrating the system around the power-generating units provided by the American company Caterpillar (of tractor fame). Gas-powered, of the total fuel energy generated only 5 per cent becomes waste energy, with the usable output being 65 per cent heat energy and 30 per cent electrical energy. Sized for optimal thermal loads (heating and chilling), and the significant levels of process heat usage (autoclaves, treatments and paint drying), energy transmissions are minimised by using hot air for mass space heating and paint drying. The system is also synchronised with the local electrical grid supply (15MVA) for reduced business interruption and decentralised locations provide energy centres close to the main thermal loads. The utilisation of warm air systems results in a 35 per cent reduction in energy consumption for the mass space heating, with even temperatures within the multi-storey building, and a better working environment for the operators and the manufactured product. It is in this context that the 'high' 37m to roof factory area was so designed to accommodate the vertical wing assembly and lifting height while the 20m 'low' horizontal wing equipping area affords considerable conservation of space heating volume. These systems also assist in mitigating some of the heat loss from opening the large factory doors during winter months and the acceleration of the recovery of temperature in the production areas. They also ensure uniform curing and the requisite quality of the wing fuel tank interior sealing. Importantly, annual savings in carbon dioxide emissions amount to around 2,700 tonnes with the ability for 'carbon trading'. Overall site electrical loading and costs are minimised, so establishing Airbus as a leading UK environmental performer. This system is now being progressively extended to embrace the whole of the Broughton site.

*The Broughton West Factory new-generation Combined Heat and Power (CHP) system.*

# Harnessing the Latest Manufacturing Methods

New 'state-of-the-art' manufacturing facilities at Broughton for the A380 wing production have included a £75 million investment for a new long-bed skin milling facility, a new automated 'creep-form' (ACF) facility to shape the curvature of the wing skin cover panels to conform with the aerofoil profile when assembled, a new stringer manufacturing centre (a 'stringer' is a spanwise stiffening member which is riveted or bolted onto the inside face of the wing skin cover panel), and new third-generation low voltage electromagnetic riveting (LVER) machines for automatic riveting of the stringers to the wing skin panels. (Other Broughton manufacturing facilities simultaneously receiving corresponding up-grades include a new A320 wing painting facility, to cut a day from flow time, and the progressive replacement of the Gemcor Drivmatic automated riveting machines originally installed for the A300 (see page 113) with new ones of the A380 technology standard.) Extensive research and development is also in progress embracing the future deployment of automotive-style robotics and rapid prototyping for tooling as well as for actual wing components.

*The new A380 wing manufacturing installations at the Broughton site. Construction in the East Factory extensions was by AMEC, the world's third largest civil engineering services group.*

Broughton has unrivalled experience in computer numerically controlled (CNC) long-bed wing skin 'machining-from-the-solid' and the new A380 skin milling extension measures 106m x 55m with a floor space of 6,340sq.m. Made by the Canadian specialist manufacturer, Henri Line, the two latest 20,000rpm twin-spindle machines are each 140ft (40m) long by 39ft (13m) wide and sculpture-machine two panels simultaneously with an cutting accuracy of 0.1mm over the full length. Together they sculpture mill 18 of the 20 skin panels on each A380 wing from single aluminium billets, the largest of which is almost 115ft (35m) long, the largest in the world. The machine beds are at floor level, a new concept to provide a safer working environment. Flat machined, the panels are held in place by vacuum suction. Previous practice was for the inside of the panels to be machined with 'facets' in order to locate material accurately where required. The innovation for the A380 panels is for these facets to be replaced with 'strip surfaces' for even better optimisation of the distribution of material for the spanwise stringer mounting lands and so also achieve lower weight, improved stringer attachment and simpler tooling. The manufacturing process has thus changed from a very complex milling exercise of different profiles and axes to a much simpler linear process. After several months of manufacturing test articles, the first cut for an A380 panel on these new long-bed machines came in December 2000 and produced from a 35m, 4.5-ton billet of aluminium alloy from which more than 75 per cent of the metal was removed with a new system for recoverable swarfage.

Working in partnership with academia and specialist manufacturing industry suppliers, Airbus has invested £18 million in the unique Broughton development of the hitherto 'laboratory-scale' automated creep-forming (ACF) technology to full production status for forming the complex double-curvature A380 wing skin cover panels to achieve the required aerodynamic profile and performance. This was because these extremely large and relatively thick top skin panels could not be formed by the conventional (originally Vickers-Weybridge developed) 'shot-peening' technique – with which all previous Airbus model wing panels are formed. The breakthrough ACF technology affords very accurate forming, eliminating the 'spring-back' problem and thereby also reducing the assembly cycle-time and cost. Made by Autoform Autoclave Systems Ltd of Dorset, and installed in the East factory, the new large-scale gas-powered 5.4 megawatt Autoclave ACF facility – in simple terms a very large oven – is 42m long by 6m diameter, has a 7-tonne door, weighs 300 tonnes, is the largest in Europe and one of the largest in the world. After extensive prior trials with some of the much smaller A320 wing panels, forming of the first A380 production panel by this method was completed in March 2003. The bottom skin panels, incorporating less curvature and being of more ductile material, are still formed by shot-peening by the long-established and now greatly extended specialist on-site American Metal Improvement Company (MIC) – a wholly owned subsidiary of the Curtiss-Wright Corporation of Roseland, New Jersey, USA (which itself has its origins with the famous American pioneer aviation signatories, Glenn Curtiss and the Wright Brothers).

The innovative modular and flexible ACF tooling concept consists of 1,200 tightly spaced carbon-steel laser-profiled rib boards with integral sensors which act as a guide system on each of the eight separate creep form tools. The flat machined aluminium wing skin panels are wrapped and clamped onto these profile boards before the whole tool enters the autoclave for vacuum forming. During the 24-hour process the panels are 'baked' to 150 degrees C (300°F) uniformly controlled to within half a degree, at a pressure of 7.5 bar (109lb/in$^2$) using eight different heating sections, the 'over-formed' panels are then unwrapped and spring back by a controlled 80 per cent to preserve their metallic qualities and retaining curvature to an accuracy of 2mm (0.08in) before being passed forward for anodizing and painting.

The new £35 million stringer manufacturing centre for machining the bottom wing skin stiffening members for the A380 (and other models) measures 344m x 82m, a floor space of 210,000 sq.m. (226,050 sq.ft). This new facility has the benefits of close-coupled manufacturing and is capable of producing stringers of up to 82ft in length and to very close tolerances of thickness to less than 0.15mm. Five production processes are involved: machining, forming, treatments, shot-peening and collation. As well as ultimately reducing cycle times, less inventory is needed resulting in corresponding cost savings. A new collation area is increasing efficiency by allowing complex sets of bottom stringers to be collated in webbing straps and delivered for assembly pre-prepared for attaching direct to the milled wing skin panels. Completed in mid-2002, production of the first A380 machined stringers began in January 2003 and the new facility can produce up to 200km of these stringers per year. Two million Euros are also being invested in a new heat treatment oven made by Pladrest of Sheffield in this centre to perform all post-machining processes for the two-thirds of the A320 family wing top stringers made in California, where they have hitherto also undergone forming, treatment and painting before being shipped to Broughton. The new facility will recover this investment within the first year of operation.

One of the four third-generation 165m-long 100t electrostatic low-voltage electronic riveter (LVER) machines supplied by Electroimpact Inc of Seattle, USA, and installed in a $50 million investment in the West Factory for the fully automatic drilling, milling, riveting, bolting and sealing of the stringers to the machined wing skin panels and developed from those earlier installed at Broughton, first for the A320 family wing manufacture and then for those of the larger A330/340 wide-body family. Altogether, the four machines can accommodate up to 16 wing skins. A high level of automation is incorporated and only two machine operators are required. There are two lines of these machines for the upper wing panels and two for the lower panels in the vertically mounted Stage 01 wing assembly jigs. Bed flatness is within 0.01mm over every 300mm and the maximum total bed flatness is within 80 microns. Each riveting/bolting 'head' services three in-line fixtures and drills and inserts rivet and lockbolt fasteners of up to half-an-inch diameter, with a faster feed system for rivets than bolts and collars, and installs a nut on the metal bolt slug. They also sense the countersink depth by measuring the hole size and stack thickness and automatically measure the need for the hole to be cold-worked and perform the process where required. With a 20,000rpm spindle speed, each produces four rivets per minute and 15,000 per skin panel with positional accuracy of 0.002in. The two types of head are: the HAWDE (Horizontal Automated Drilling Equipment and pronounced 'howdy'), a five axis machine which glides along two rails, one metre above the other, and can drill a perfect hole every eight seconds at right angles to any area of the wing skin; and the GRAWDE (Gear Rib Automatic Wing Drilling Equipment and pronounced 'growdy') used to drill 1,500 holes per wing set from 15mm to 25mm through the very thick wing skin, the landing gear rib and the inner rear spar area. Process data to run these machines is translated direct from the CADDS5 (Computer-Aided Design Drafting System) data. These machines reduce fastening times by up to two thirds – a saving of 10 days over the previous manual process of locating heavy drill templates and large rack feed drills.

*The Airbus A380 'show-the-workforce' flyover of the new Airbus UK Broughton 'West Factory' on 18 May 2006, and where its wings were built.*

*Overhead the Airbus UK Broughton wing manufacturing complex of today with (lower left) the original, and now much up-dated, 'East Factory', (lower right) the several recent specialist extensions, and (upper centre) the new 'West Factory', separated by the also much improved Hawarden Airfield main runway. (cf the similar views of the site in July 1947 on page 38 and in August 2000 on page 124).*

# Eleven

# Building the World's Largest Airliner Wings

Embodying the same general three-spar layout as all of its predecessors, but with most ribs perpendicular to the rear spar almost to the root and many of them being of composite construction, hybrid metallic/composite flap beams, trussed leading edge ribs and numerous other new features, the design and manufacture of the A380 wing structure – much the largest (and heaviest) ever built for a commercial passenger-carrying aircraft – also had to accommodate significant scalar constraints of airport infrastructure, the control of the aircraft fuel usage requirements, and those devolving from the emergency evacuation provisions from the double-deck passenger accommodation, none of which had previously been encountered with its predecessors. Full account also had to be taken of the corresponding manufacturing implications, in particular in relation to the machining and forming of the much larger, thicker and complex double-curvature skin panels. Accordingly, wide-ranging research and development was instituted to harness the latest lean fabrication concepts to deliver significant reductions in cost, weight and production cycle-times. All of this involved the implementation of the latest techniques in computer-aided engineering (CAE) – notably using the Airbus-wide CADDS5 (Computer-Aided Design and Drafting Services System) provided by the Parametric Technology Corporation (PTC), together with knowledge-based engineering (KBE) and non-linear finite element modeling – to fulfil much the most ambitious and formidable wing design and manufacturing assignment yet undertaken anywhere in the world.

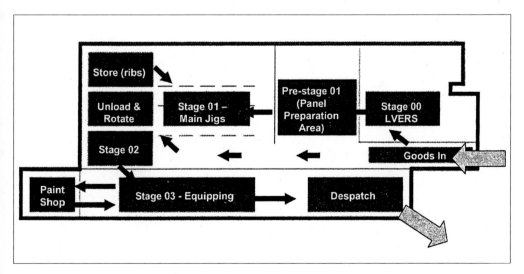

*The Broughton West Factory plant layout and A380 wing manufacturing process stages. The factory layout is a typical 'U-shaped' production line system – with one 'back flow' process, the paint shop due to potential fire risk and the ability to create a natural fire wall.*

# Evolution of the A380 Wing Aerodynamic and Structural Design

The very formidable task with which Airbus UK was beset with the design and manufacture of the A380 wing can be appreciated by a brief resume of the principal aerodynamic and structural design considerations and features.

## Aerodynamic Definition

In gestation as the A3XX first defined in October 1993, the definitive A380 aircraft design was frozen in 2000. In order to meet the very challenging performance (particularly airfield) targets, the principle objective and focus of the aerodynamic design was that the drag had to be significantly reduced compared to earlier Airbus designs.

The sheer dimensional scale of the aircraft also exposed the fundamental design constraint that it had to be sized to fit within the internationally agreed '80m (260ft) square box' airport ramp area. The resulting wing design then devolved from a complex trade-off between speed, fuel volume, and the use of simple landing flaps. From the original, independent wing submissions by the four Airbus partners, the then British Aerospace Filton concept was selected – with full collaborative development incorporating all wing experience throughout the Airbus partnership.

Hence the design lineage stemmed from the original Airbus A300/A310 wing devised by Hawker Siddeley at Hatfield, and benefiting from the earlier de havilland Comet, HS/BAE Nimrod and Trident; and the A320, for which the British Aerospace-Weybridge team (with their strong input from the Vickers VC10 and BAC One-Eleven) originally held the aerodynamic design responsibility. When Airbus wing design in the UK was being transferred from BAe-Hatfield to Filton in 1984, the latter team then assumed overall responsibility for the A3XX wing. They had also worked on the final refinement of the original Weybridge-designed A320 wing and the Hatfield-designed A330/A340 wing, but the A3XX wing was the first opportunity to exercise fully their own skills, albeit strongly based on the heritage  from their Hatfield and Weybridge predecessors.

The definitive A380 wing was deliberately sized to accommodate an eventual 20 per cent stretch in aircraft capacity – with an overall area of 845sq.m. The span was then fixed at 79.8m to comply not only with the '80m box' limitation but also with those placed on the root chord. This latter dimension had to be less than 60ft (18.3m) to comply with American Federal Aviation Administration (FAA) rules governing the maximum distance between passenger exits and the provision of adequate space for the deployment of emergency escape slides from both passenger decks. The mean sweepback is 33.5 degrees. The inboard trailing-edge 'kink' resulted from the usual one of the need to accommodate the main undercarriage pintle mounting and stowage arrangements behind the main structural box. The aerodynamic design aim was again the conventional one of providing as much sweep as possible on the inboard section while endeavouring to reduce the sweep outboard. The final shape and size of the 2.4m high winglets was based on the BAe-patented A320 design and determined using theorems originally developed by the famous German theoretical aerodynamicist, Max Munk. The required margin for growth in capacity was preserved by ensuring enough wing area to support the corresponding higher design weights and sufficient fuel volume. The total fuel capacity is 310,000 litres (83,000 US gal) – around 6,200 times that of a typical 50-litre capacity motor car.

A critical and late-arising take-off and landing performance requirement was the ability to meet the London-Heathrow Quota Count (QC) noise rules. This resulted not only in the need for bigger engines and the reworking of the wing to accommodate them, but also in the adoption of a droop-nose device (DND) as originally developed for the HS Trident – a patented variable-position, permanently sealed, leading-edge droop section near the wing root to improve the lift/drag ratio in order that the climb-out gradient could be improved and so provide the requisite margin relative to the QC targets.

Externally, the most distinctive visual aspect of the A380 wing is the pronounced 'gulling' shape and dihedral, together needed for a combination of aircraft stability requirements and adequate engine ground clearance, including excessive 'rolling' of the undercarriage. Before take-off, fuel is pumped between the wing and the tailplane trim tanks (i.e. longitudinal transfers) in order to locate the centre of gravity (CG) in the most advantageous position to minimise drag during the cruise (a la the Anglo-French Concorde). Also, after take-off, fuel is pumped outboard, and then just before landing is pumped inboard (i.e. lateral transfers), providing bending moment relief and 'active' load alleviation to the outboard wing. in order to reduce fatigue loads.

Further significant wing bending load and moment relief was achieved by taking a cue from the original pioneering of wing load alleviation for commercial air transport in passive form with the Vickers VC10, which used symmetric aileron up-float at high operating weights. Airbus introduced 'active' load alleviation in this way on the A330, with fuselage-mounted accelerometers triggering rapid aileron and spoiler deflection in up-gusts to reduce the applied gust loads and this feature has also been applied to the A380 with three-section independently operated up-floating ailerons.

The weight of the A380 wing structure was reduced by incorporating inverse camber in the root section (again a la the Vickers VC10) so moving the span loading inboard past the aerodynamic ideal of elliptical loading, which saved around 3.5 tonnes. The most sophisticated computational fluid dynamics (CFD) and three-dimensional optimisation analyses were deployed to gain approximately two per cent in drag improvement, in offset, so restoring the original design drag at the typical cruising speed of Mach 0.85 and the maximum operating Mach Number of 0.89.

# Structural Design

The A380 airframe structure has a design service life goal of 19,000 flight cycles and 140,000 flying hours or 25 years, whichever is sooner. The cantilever three-spar main wing comprises the Broughton-built primary load-carrying torsion box structure/integrally sealed main fuel tankage, an inboard fixed leading edge and support structure for the slats and droop nose sections forward of the inner front spar, and an attachment structure behind the rear spar for the flaps, spoilers and ailerons as well as the main landing gear pintle housing. Within the main box structure are housed additional supports for the engine pylons, flap support beams and main landing gear. Each wing supports six leading edge slats and two droop nose sections, three aileron sections and eight spoiler/speed brakes. The inner wing box contains three spars front, centre and aft – made from either 7085 or 7040 advanced aluminium alloy, with the centre spar acting as a fuel tank dividing wall. Upper and lower skins comprise twenty machined panels with separate stingers and are made from 7449 and 7055 (upper) and 2024hdt and 2026 (lower) aluminium alloys – dictated by static and fatigue strength, and fatigue and damage tolerance considerations respectively. The forward skin panels extend slightly ahead of the front spar to provide attachment for the fixed leading-edge structure, while at the rear spar they extend aft locally as far as the main landing gear pintle forging. Spars and ribs are both metallic and composite (78 and 48 respectively) – the first use of composite ribs as primary structure on this scale – for cost and weight reasons. Metallic ribs are used in highly loaded areas such as the fuel tank boundaries, pylon and landing gear support, while most of the inboard ribs are also metallic for crashworthiness reasons. This hybrid metallic/composite rib construction has resulted in a substantial weight saving. Flap track beams are of metal/composite construction. The centre fuselage carry-through box structure consists of aluminium alloy and carbon-fibre reinforced plastic (CFRP). Also incorporated are a number of structural heritage legacy features, notably in the extreme outer (thinner-skinned) wing section which consists of two spars and integrally machined skin/stringer panels largely based on the design and manufacturing heritage of the Vickers Vanguard, VC10 and BAC One-Eleven built at Weybridge in the late 1950s and the 1960s – and from Concorde. The enormous size of the A380 wing structure is typically demonstrated by the fact that it takes almost a minute to walk from the tip to the root and the deepest section of the wing root is almost 3m – more then a standing man.

# The A380 Wing Assembly Process

Around a quarter of the component parts for the A380 wing are fabricated in the Broughton East Factory, the remainder coming from 400 suppliers and several large global suppliers: notably including Mecachrome, France: centre spar; Airbus UK Filton: rear spar assembly, main landing gear rib and other ribs; Airbus Espana: carbon-fibre ribs; CAV (California, USA): stringers; Saab of Sweden: mid and outer fixed leading edges; Spirit AeroSystems (ex-BAE Systems at Prestwick, Scotland): inner fixed leading edge structure; and GKN Isle of Wight: trailing edge secondary structure. The extreme outer wing incorporates Broughton-made integrally machined top skin/stringer panels (by Ingersoll cutter) and the bottom equivalents are Korean made. The Broughton West Factory houses the main wing box assembly jigs and equipping area, where all 'non-moveables' and fuel, hydraulic, electrical, pneumatic and anti-icing systems are installed and tested before painting and delivery. Each complete wing set comprises 32,000 parts – with additional assemblies from Belairbus (Belgium): leading edge moving devices; Airbus Deutschland: flaps; and Airbus France: spoilers/ailerons, being added at the aircraft final assembly stage at Toulouse.

Stage 00: Stringer Attachment. After receiving surface treatment by the Metal Improvement Company (MIC) the machined wing skin panels are treated to prevent corrosion before they reach the sub-assembly area for the attachment of the machined and formed stiffening stringers – seen here in place for automatic riveting and bolting by the low voltage electromagnetic riveter (LVER) machines. Each wing incorporates 314 stringers, 124 for the top wing skins and 190 for the bottom skins. It is at this stage that the fuel tank interior sealing process begins with a Thiokol sealant interface applied between the stringer face and the inner surface of the skin panel.

Above, left: *Stage 01: Main Structural Assembly. After the Pre-Stage 01 (panel preparation ) area, this area comprises four vertically mounted wing torsion box structural assembly jigs (design and supplied by Hyde of Manchester and Electroimpact of the USA), with five levels of staging for operator access, each jig holding a port and a starboard unit. The pre-assembled leading, centre and trailing edge spars and ribs are assembled first before the skin/stringer panels are located. First the bottom and then the top skins are drilled off and removed for de-burring and replacement for final bolt-up. The huge one-piece wing root rib measures 7 metres in length and 2.5 metres at its minimum height. The fuel tank sealing process continues progressively with the fillet sealant applied to the stringer edges and at all of the bolted skin panel, spar and rib attachment interfaces.*

Above, right:*The final 'bolt-up' of the pre-assembled and riveted skin/stringer panels. 750,000 fasteners (bolts, nuts and rivets) are incorporated during the construction of each wing set.*

*The main landing gear pintle support forging attached to the junction of the heavy-duty landing gear rib and the rear of the wing trailing-edge spar. This huge structural component is machined by GE Aviation (formerly Smiths Aerospace) of Hamble, near Southampton, the modern-day successor to the Folland Aircraft Company there which was a major supplier to the original Vickers-Chester Wellington production line.*

141

*Stage 02: Removal from the Assembly Jig and Geometric Assessment. The first A380 wing torsion box structure removed from the assembly jig on 4 November 2003. The jig unloading process involves the release of a single large bolt whence the back of the jig is opened up and the five working decks and tooling structure are retracted. The wing structure is then lifted vertically via the installed engine pylon attachment forks and turned to the horizontal orientation, placed on an inflatable hovercraft-type system, which is an integral part of the assembly jig, before being measured for root end volume and other key geometric datum points and transferred to the wing equipping area.*

*Stage 03: Wing Equipping. At the second bend of the 'U-shaped' factory layout, the first A380 wing was moved into this area on 12 November 2003 where four sets of wings are accommodated for the fitting of the externally supplied leading- and trailing-edge substructures, the hybrid metal composite flap track support beams (each with its own lift because of size and weight) and the installation of the aircraft operating systems wiring, piping and ducting. The full wing equipping stage involves the installation of 360,000 metres (223.6 miles of wiring, piping and ducting. The high-pressure 5,000psi hydraulic system installation – the first for a civil aircraft (cf the previous standard hydraulic system pressure of 3,000psi) – has resulted in reduced pipe sizes and correspondingly smaller amounts of hydraulic fluid required.*

# Twelve

# Transport Logistics

Materials handling and production 'transport' at the Chester/Broughton site has embraced four sequential modal phases. Traditionally building and maintaining complete fly-away aircraft during its first 30 years, the principal 'in-house' transport facility during that time was the original overhead craneage system which continues in use for Airbus wing transport in the East Factory to this day – albeit in much modified form with 20-ton cranes and now controllable from floor level. In recent years, this system has been augmented by the use of purpose-designed 'hovercraft-type' inflatable air-bag pallet vehicles for transferring the much larger and heavier A330/340 and A380 wing structures (in the East and West factories respectively) from their vertically assembled position into the horizontal position for equipping. However, when Hawker Siddeley designated Chester as the Airbus wing manufacturing centre in 1970, a whole new mode was required to transport these very large structures to their continental European equipping and final assembly centres – initially Toulouse and later also Bremen. First, this was the turboprop-powered 'Super Guppy' adaptation of the Boeing Stratocruiser transport and military tanker, with its greatly enlarged fuselage originally devised to transport major sections of the American Saturn IV rocket system across the USA. When these aircraft became 'time-expired', and the much increased production activity demanded, Airbus then devised a specially adapted equivalent version of its own A300-600 – the A300-600ST Super Transporter 'Beluga' – with sufficient capacity to accommodate all Airbus family wings up to and including the A340-500/600 Series. The exceptional scale of the A380 wings, too large and heavy to be accommodated by the Beluga, then demanded a correspondingly new multi-modal transport system (MMTS). This land- and water-borne transport system is integrated with the transfer of major fuselage and tail unit sections from the German, French and Spanish manufacturing centres to the final assembly at Toulouse – the first time that the aerospace industry has implemented such a transport system. The shipping of Airbus assemblies across Europe is often seen as inefficient. In fact, the distances traveled in Europe (e.g. Broughton to Toulouse, 870nm) are little different to transporting Boeing 747 fuselage sections from Northrop, California, to Seattle, 830nm; for 737 empennages from Wichita, Kansas, or Japan to Seattle (1,342 and 5,400nm respectively). All four transport modes have also been complemented by a large range of purpose-built in-house movement mechanisms, together with road transport trailers and scissor-lift devices.

*Overleaf, top: One of the two free-ranging five-ton overhead 'Royce' cranes installed in the original Vickers-Chester Shadow Factory for the movement of wartime aircraft wings and engines into place for final assembly to fuselages moved on ground trolleys until the complete aircraft could be moved on their own undercarriages. This original system continued to serve well into the post-war era, with the ability to lift complete fighter aircraft and the fuselages and wings of the much larger and heavier Comet in the late 1950s and early 1960s, as seen here, and using conventional pulleys, beams, slings, shackles and hooks. The latest ground-controlled DEMAG heavy duty (20-ton) overhead cranes now permeate the West Factory and all the new extensions in the East Factory.*

*The signal event of the first set of Hawker Siddeley Aviation Chester-built wings for the initiating Airbus A300B airliner being loaded aboard an Aeromaritime/Airbus Industrie 'Super Guppy' specialist freighter aircraft on 23 November 1971 at Manchester Airport from a custom-designed scissor-lift trailer and bound for (what was then) the VFW Factory at Bremen, Germany, for equipping prior to onward flight to the Aerospatiale Factory at Toulouse in south-west France, for final assembly. This voluminous aircraft was a turboprop-powered adaptation of the original Boeing Stratocruiser transport/military tanker with a hinged-nose loading facility and was long used for the international transport of Airbus airframe components around Europe.*

# The Super Guppy Freighter

Seeking a solution for the redeployment of surplus Boeing Stratocruisers, an aircraft broker and an imaginative designer, Jack Conroy, saw an increasing opportunity in the 1960s for suitable aircraft to be used to carry very high-value outsize loads and came up with the radically enlarged (19ft diameter) upper fuselage, hinged-tail unit, conversion. Their effort was, in fact, directed solely at the trans-America transport requirement of the American National Aeronautics and Space Agency (NASA), hitherto forced to transit its bulky space rocket booster cases from the Douglas Factory in California by sea through the Panama Canal and across the Gulf of Mexico to the launch base at Cape Canaveral (later renamed Cape Kennedy) in Florida, a 2,700-mile journey taking several weeks. So was the 'Pregnant Guppy' borne (the name 'Guppy' deriving from the fat and ungainly fish of that name). Conversion work by the specialist company, On-Mark Engineering, at Van Nuys, California, began in November 1961 The first of these giant freighters was first flown on 19 September 1963 before beginning service in the late Summer of 1963 by Aero Spacelines. So successful was it – in the 1970s it was notably used for the aerial inter-site transport of the fully equipped airframe components for the Anglo-French Concorde – that an even larger version, the turboprop-powered 'Super Guppy', with a cargo load carrying capacity of 24,494kg (53,000lb) over a range of 900nm (1,035 miles), followed, this time with a hinged-nose loading facility, and was widely used by the American aerospace industry. When Airbus Industrie faced a similar problem to NASA, this was again the only suitable aircraft available, and the Van Nuys Factory was commissioned to build two more aircraft for its pan-European air transport operation, such that no major component would be 'out-of-work time' for more than a maximum of 48 hours. However, when the vaulting Airbus production tempo required extra capacity, Aero Spacelines had ceased trading. Airbus therefore purchased the rights to the Super Guppy design and contracted the French air operating company, Aeromaritime (a UTA subsidiary), to build and operate a further two aircraft and to operate the whole Airbus inter-factory 'in-house airline' operation. When Airbus finally retired the Super Guppy fleet (with one being acquired by NASA), it had logged more then 47,000 hours during its twenty-five-year life.

# The Airbus Super Transporter 'Beluga' Freighter

When in 1990 it was clear that the aging Super Guppy fleet would have to be replaced, Airbus decided that a new-generation equivalent could be developed using its own reliable A300-600R airframe (incorporating Broughton-made wings) and on 22 August 1991 approved the construction

*One of the fleet of five specially designed Airbus A300-600ST 'Super Transporter' aircraft into which the Broughton-made wing structures are now loaded from a custom-built elevated platform via a clam-shell nose-loading door on the main deck above the low-mounted flight deck for main airframe component transport to the Airbus continental European final assembly centres in France and Germany as appropriate.*

of four of these 'Super Transporters' with an option on a fifth. Developed and manufactured by the Special Airbus Transport International Company (SATIC), a joint subsidiary of the then French Aerospatiale-Matra Airbus and German DaimlerChrysler Aerospace Airbus, and nicknamed 'Beluga' (due to its resemblance to the great white whale of that name), the first aircraft was first flown in September 1994, the second in March 1996, the third in April 1997, the fourth in July 1998 and the fifth in 1999. After 12 months of flight development, the first of this distinctive new type began the progressive replacement of the Super Guppy fleet from October 1997. To facilitate the preferred 'straight-in' nose loading, without the complication of breaking and recalibration of systems between each flight with the Super Guppy type hinged-nose design, the elegant solution was to mount the flight deck below the level of the cargo hold floor and to install a large but conventional upward-opening clam-shell type cargo door to allow direct access to the (unpressurised) hold. Incorporating an extended A340 tail section, the aircraft was also fitted with tailplane endplate fins for improved directional stability. Currently the world's most voluminous cargo aircraft, it can transport twice the load of the Super Guppy. The massively enlarged hold has a usable length of 123ft 8in (37.70m), 24.3ft (7.4m) width and a total volume of 49,440cuft (1,400cum), enabling 105,310lb (45.5 tonnes) to be transported over a range of 4,630km (2,500nm). For Broughton, currently manufacturing and delivering 57 wing sets per month (42 single-aisle and 15 long-range), this volumetric capacity is sufficient to transport two sets of wing boxes for the A320/A321/A319/ A318 Series, one set for the A300/A330/A340 Series, or single wings for the A340-500/600 Series and now the A350XWB. Constructed in the Sogerma plant at Bordeaux-Merignac, and again operated by Aeromarime on behalf of Airbus, these aircraft now visit Broughton up to three times each working day, with turnaround times of approximately one hour. The Beluga's ability to transport very large and sensitive cargo means that it is in high demand from other companies and is also marketed by Air Transport International (ATI), an Airbus subsidiary formed in 1996, which leases these aircraft when not in their primary use for the Airbus production cycle and has undertaken wide-ranging outsize cargo charters, including space vehicle components on both sides of the Atlantic

# A380 Wing Transportation

The major new Airbus industrial saga that began on 19 December 2000, with the official launch of the new giant generation A380 company flagship, not only required the uniquely audacious A3XX design concept to be translated into hardware reality in about forty months but also portended the extremely demanding prospect of building the means of production and establishing a transport infrastructure and logistics network through the same manufacturing centres of excellence on a correspondingly giant scale. Because the Super Transporter did not have the capacity to convey A380 wings and other sub-assemblies, which were too large and heavy, before deciding on the definitive surface-transport solution, various other possible aerial delivery methods were evaluated, including a 'piggyback' on the A340. Taking inspiration from the method developed by NASA – for transporting the American Space Shuttle from its landing site at Edwards Air Force base to Cape Canaveral 'piggybacked' on a specially adapted Boeing 747 – the French space agency, CNES, had earlier seriously considered transporting the European spacecraft, Hermes, on top of a modified Airbus A300B. However, the Hermes programme was cancelled long before the idea could become a reality. There was also the Russian example of the transport of space vehicles being launched from the Baikonur Space Centre by a Myasishchyev 3M Bison strategic bomber and the sole Antonov AN-225 Mriya ('Dream'), by far the heaviest and most powerful aircraft ever built, thought to have been specifically designed to carry the (later moribund) Buran Space shuttle on its back. However, all of these 'piggyback' possibilities were abandoned because they would have only been suitable for wing transport alone.

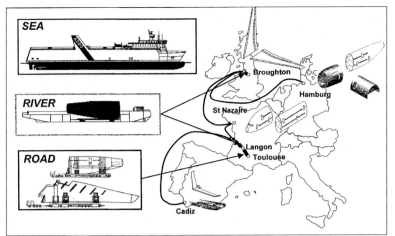

The innovative multi-modal integrated Europe-wide A380 transportation system that was eventually devised by Airbus embraced road, river and open sea segments. The first A380 wing delivery from the West Factory via this system was made on Tuesday 6 April 2004.

*The first A380 equipped wing structure leaving the dispatch bay of the West Factory on the custom-designed multi-purpose vehicle (MPV) manufactured in France by Nicholas – a 12-line, 96-wheel, trailer capable of carrying 140 tonnes (the weight of one wing and its transportation jig). Fitted with optical, wire and visual guidance systems to enable it to negotiate the similarly equipped initial 1.6km road route to the barge 'load-out' dock on the nearby River Dee, this somewhat circuitous route was pre-surveyed on 28 March 2004, using a representative dummy wing space model under load, notably to check the transit and loading of the Bridge 18a over the Crewe-Chester-Holyhead railway line.*

Overleaf, top: *Safely and expeditiously transiting Bridge 18a – a particularly delicate operation because the maximum loading of the bridge was 200 tonnes and it had to take the wing with a total weight, including the MPV and travel jig, of 198 tonnes. The wing (with heavy protective coverings on the leading and trailing edge secondary structures) also had to be parked on the bridge for a time and the deflections carefully measured. The planning and preparation in conjunction with Network Rail had to be extremely thorough and diligent and necessitated the provision of numerous safety features to obviate the possibility of debris falling onto the tracks. Fortunately, the whole exercise was satisfactorily completed without the need for a new bridge to be constructed, which would have added a considerable and unwanted delay and cost to the A380 programme.*

Left: *The 'load-out' transfer from road trailer to river barge at the berth on the River Dee. The river is very 'tidal' and can change by more than 2m in as little as 20 minutes. The schedule for wing dispatch is therefore very much tide-dependant to pass under bridges but also has to be timed very accurately to avoid running aground. However, the craft is designed to run aground with safety and in nautical terms this is known as a NABSA (normally afloat but safe aground) design.*

Opposite above: *Navigating the A380 wing along the River Dee aboard the specially designed Dee River Craft (DRC), 'Afon Dyfrowy', on the short journey to the Port of Mostyn for transfer to the open-sea going vessel and the onward journey to its intermediate continental European destinations en-route to the final assembly at Toulouse. Custom-built by McTay Marine Ltd of Bromborough, Merseyside, this barge was first 'floated out' on 10 February 2004. An open-deck, flat-bottom vessel, and suitable for river navigation only, it is specially fitted with 'bull bars' to protect the wing structure if the tide is too high when the craft is passing under bridges. Interestingly, this first phase of the wing delivery journey delivery also involves 'history revisited' by recalling the origins of its Broughton birthplace when passing under the historic Queensferry Bridge spanning the River Dee which was built in 1926 by the famed civil engineering contractor, Sir William Arrol and Son, who built the original Vickers-Chester Shadow Factory in 1939.*

The purpose-designed 'Ville de Bordeaux' open-sea 'roll-on roll-off' container ship – taking its name from its French sea port destination and proudly and prominently labeled 'Airbus A380 on board' – is the backbone of the A380 airframe delivery logistics chain. Built in the Chinese Jinling shipyard in Nanjing province, the vessel is 154 metres long, 24 metres wide and features the largest-ever watertight stern door (22m wide by 14m deep) on such a vessel. Commissioned by FRET/Cetam, a subsidiary of Louis Dreyfus Armateurs of France and Leif Hoegh of Norway, it is chartered by Airbus. Jinjing won the shipbuilding contract in March 2002 in Paris, beating competition from Spain and the Republic of Korea. The vessel was launched in 2003 and delivered in March 2004. Visiting five ports in four countries, it transports wings, fuselage and tail sections from their individual assembly sites – Hamburg (Germany), St Nazaire (France) and Seville (Spain) respectively – in every rotation to Bordeaux. At Mostyn, precision timing of the transfer operation requires the barge to be moored at high tide and as the water falls it comes to rest on a platform that perfectly aligns it with the ramp of the ferry ship so that the wings can be moved aboard safely.

The A380 wing and transport trailer inside the cavernous hold of the 'Ville de Bordeaux'. On arrival at its namesake port, the final part of the journey of its multiple cargo across France consists of first navigating the Garonne river, again by flat top barge (made by Dutch builder, De Hoop), to Langon, before transferring to road transport again.

A pair of Broughton-made wings on the last leg of their delivery journey in the 'oversize itinerary' road convoy, singly in the tilted position, en-route to the A380 Clement Ader final assembly centre at the EADS Jean-Luc-Lagardere Factory complex at Toulouse-Blagnac. As at the start, this final sector of the delivery route was facilitated by extensive prior dummy space model checking runs and road construction work, particularly the re-routing of the RD963.

The first Airbus UK Broughton-built A380 wings at the threshold of becoming airborne under their own lift with the maiden flight of the first aircraft (MSN001), powered by four British-built Rolls-Royce Trent 900 engines at Toulouse on 27 April 2005 for 3 hours 54 minutes – thirty-eight months from the first ground-breaking for the Broughton West Factory in August 2001. (© AIRBUS S.A.S. 2005  - photo by exm company/ P. Masclet)

# The Airbus Airliner Wing Family Product Line

Six successive and distinct wing torsion box structures have been designed and built for the comprehensive range of airliners which Airbus offers today – embracing twelve principal models from 107 to 555 seats capacity and up to a maximum range of 8,500nm – developed since the original A300 concept gave birth to the four-nation European Airbus partnership in 1970 and for which Broughton has been the exclusive supplier from the outset. This is its distinctive contribution to the creation of a complete European industrial enterprise and infrastructure without equal and producing this full family of high-technology airliners with almost exponential growth, global market competitiveness and success. Moreover, these aircraft offer the unique benefit of a common flightdeck concept throughout and so facilitating Cross Crew Qualification (CCQ) and mixed fleet flying (MFF) to allow any pilot to transition from any one type to any other in the entire Airbus range with minimum training.

The founding 300-seat (hence the designation) A300 concept – the world's first twin-aisle twin – was actually realised in hardware as the smaller 250-seat A300B based on the expressed requirements of the two 'home customers', Air France and Germany's Lufthansa. The first example first flew on 29 October 1972 and the new type first entered service with Air France in May 1974. A small technical change to the wing root resulted in the A300-B2, which was shortly followed by the slightly larger -B4. This, in turn, was followed by the 266-seat A300-600, which was first flown nine years later on 8 July 1983, and later the -600F (Freighter).

When in March 1978 Eastern Airlines of the USA took the revolutionary step of agreeing to lease four A300-B4s for the airline's key New York-Miami route – basically rent-free and only paying for training, fuel and spares, with Airbus paying for the maintenance for six months – an invaluable early foothold was gained in the key American domestic market and in the absence at that time of a home-grown equivalent. After the airline had ordered 23 aircraft with options on nine more, it then stated a requirement for what was to become the smaller A310 (but which ironically it never actually ordered). From then onwards, the A300 began to sell well, particularly to the rapidly expanding Asian market, making Airbus a credible new force in the global commercial aircraft marketplace. The 220-seat A310 was launched in July 1978 which, as Airbus had originally intended, was to begin the start of a family lineage.

By the mid-1970s, it was becoming clear that the prolific 140-170 Boeing 727 and 120-seat Douglas DC9 regional jets would need to be replaced. This resulted in the start of a new branch of the Airbus family – with the 150-seat single-aisle A320 which was launched in March 1984. Its main selling point was its much more advanced technology, most notably its breakthrough-technology, computerised, fully digital, full-authority, fly-by-wire (FBW) flight control system, designed to prevent pilots from being able to exceed the flight envelope inadvertently, either in stalling or at excessive speeds, which could cause structural damage, and which its competitors did not possess until much later. Additionally, the A320 incorporated an all-digital two-pilot 'glass cockpit', that had been incorporated into the A310 and the A300-600. (The last of the 822 A300/A310 aircraft was delivered on 12 July 2007.)

The decision to launch the 185-seat A321 came on 24 November 1989 and the smaller 124-seat A319 on 10 June 1993. A reorientation of work-sharing between the French and German partners then resulted in the production of the prolifically selling A320 family being built at Toulouse while the three derivatives – the A321, A319 and (later also) the 107-seat A318 – became virtually German-built aircraft, built at Finkenwerder, along the River Elbe from Hamburg. Today, more than 6,000 A320/A321/A319/A318 wing sets have been completed and delivered for these best-selling single-aisle aircraft.

Meanwhile, Airbus had been considering a larger, longer-range version of the baseline A300 and in early 1986 began developing what was to become the 253 to 335-seat A330/A340 twin- and four-engine twin-aisle siblings as advanced technology aircraft that could replace the A300 and A310 and which were launched on 5 June 1987. The A330/A340 would also have fly-by-wire controls and a glass cockpit. The A340 flew first in October 1991 and the structurally similar A330 followed in

November 1992. The 'Longer-Larger-Farther-Faster-Higher-Quieter-Smoother' 380-seat A340-600 development with an ingenious new wing was launched in December 1997 and first flown in April 2001, followed by its extra long-range 313-seat -500 sibling in February 2002.

First announced in conceptual form as the A3XX in 1996, the giant 555-passenger A380 was officially launched on 9 December 2000 as the Airbus Flagship for the twenty-first century. The world's largest commercial aircraft, and completing the upper end of the Airbus product line without replacing any other, although of 35 per cent larger capacity, it retains similar overall dimensions to its largest predecessor, the 416-seat Boeing 747-400, and airport ramp area requirements and hence its double-deck passenger accommodation. It also has a thirteen per cent fuel consumption advantage (burning less than three litres per passenger over 100 kilometres – comparable with the best small modern turbo-diesel cars) and a 15-20 per cent seat mile cost advantage. The projected freight version will also be the world's largest cargo aircraft, with a 560-ton maximum gross take-off weight, giving it roughly a 30-ton advantage over the Russian Antonov 225 freighter.

The quantum-step A380 is arguably the first revolutionary rather than evolutionary jetliner to enter the market in 40 years, joining company with the Boeing 747 and Anglo-French Concorde, both of which were developed in the late 1960s. Launched on 1 December 2006, the first wings for the new generation Airbus A350XWB built in non-metallic carbon-fibre composite in the new Broughton North Factory were delivered in September 2012 and the first aircraft made its maiden flight at Toulouse–Blagnac on 14 June 2013, beginning a five-aircraft, 2,500-hour, certification and pre-service flight test programme.

*Size and Weight no Object: The boldly titled: 'FIRST AIRBUS A340 WING FROM BRITISH AEROSPACE-CHESTER' leaving by road for onward delivery by aerial transport in June 1990 – half way through the thirty-five-year European Airbus saga to date. The huge scale and weight (since considerably eclipsed by the A380 wing) and the custom-designed 115ft-long transport vehicle are graphically indicative of the massive and continuous additional investment that has been required across the whole Chester/Broughton Airbus wing manufacturing operation beyond that for the actual production process – and now including Airbus's own designed and built fleet of aerial freighter aircraft and specially commissioned water-borne transport vessels.*

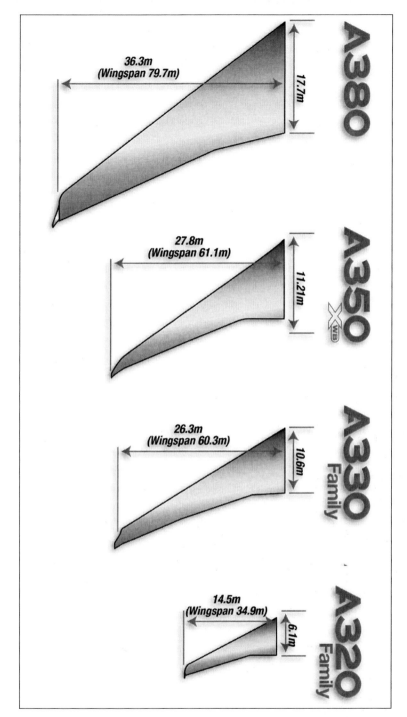

# Airbus Wing Size Comparisons

In terms of wing span, the A380 is over twice as a large as the A318 and 25 per cent bigger than the A340-500/600, is largest Airbus Predecessor.

The almost exponential growth of the Airbus airliner family is evidenced by the timeline of the first flights of each successive new type: 1972: A300B; 1982: A310; 1987: A320; 1991: A340; 1992: A330; 1993: A321; 1995: A319; 1997: A330-200; 2001: A340-600; 2002: A318 and A340-500; 2005: A380; 2013: A350XWB.

# Airbus Wing Manufacturing Milestones

The progressive build-up of Airbus wing manufacture at Chester, since the first A300 wing set was delivered on 23 November 1971 – through the thirty-six-year Hawker Siddeley/British Aerospace/ BAE Systems/Airbus UK continuum – to meet the ever-increasing number of customer orders and the continually diversifying Airbus airliner family has paralleled the evolution and global success of the whole Airbus enterprise. All twin-aisle aircraft wings (A300/A310/A330/A340) have been delivered to the German Airbus manufacturing centre at Bremen for equipping, before onward air transport to the Airbus final assembly centre at Toulouse. The first wing set for the single-aisle regional A320 was despatched from Chester to BAe Filton, Bristol, on 28 November 1985 to a new Wing Equipping Center there, before onward transport to Toulouse. This continued until July 1993 with the completion of the 453rd A320/A321 wing set, whence the equipping of these wings was reverted to Chester, before despatch to the Airbus final assembly centres at Toulouse and Hamburg respectively (also including the A319 since April 1995 and the A318 since August 2001 to Hamburg). The first A380 wing set left Broughton by surface transport on 5 April 2004. The 3,000th single aisle (A320 family) wing set was delivered on 8 November 2006 and the 5,000th Airbus family wing set (i.e. 10,000 individual wings) was delivered on 31 August 2007.

| | |
|---|---|
| 1971 August | First A300 wing box out-of-jig. |
| 1971 November | First A300 wing set despatched to VFW in Bremen for equipping. |
| 1979 June | Delivery of the 100th A300 wing set to Bremen. |
| 1981 January | 150th Airbus wing set delivered. |
| 1981 May | First A310 wing box delivered. |
| 1985 July | Assembly of the first A320 wing started. |
| 1985 September | First A320 wing removed from the assembly jig. |
| 1985 November | First A320 wing set leaves for BAe Filton for equipping, testing and completion. |
| 1989 August | 500th set of A300/A310 wings despatched to Bremen (329 A300s and 171 A310s). |
| 1990 June | First A340 wings removed from assembly jig and despatched to Bremen. |
| 1991 August | First A330 wing set removed from the assembly jig. |
| 1991 September | New £3.2 million Wing Despatch Centre opened and first A330 wing despatched. |
| 1992 March | First A321 wing removed from assembly jig. |
| 1993 July | 453rd and last wing set equipping completed at Filton. |

| | |
|---|---|
| 1994 September | First metal cut for the A319 wing. |
| 1994 November | 100th A330/A340 wing set delivered. |
| 1994 December | 500th A320 wing set delivered. |
| 1995 October | First loading of an A340 wing set into the A300-600T SuperTransporter 'Beluga' aircraft. |
| 1999 February | 2,000th Airbus wing set delivered. |
| 2000 September | Decision announced that A3XX wings to be built at Broughton. |
| 2001 April | Start of second phase of Automated Wing Box Assembly (AWBAI) project begun in 1999. First flight of A340-600 at Toulouse. |
| 2001 August | Delivery of first set of A318 wings. |
| 2001 August | Major new facility construction work started for A380 wing manufacture. |
| 2002 February | Delivery of the 3,000th Airbus wing set. |
| 2002 December | The 500th A330/A340 wing set out-of-jig. Broughton machines the first A380 wing skin panel. |
| 2003 January | New A380 manufacturing developments in the East Factory opened. |
| 2003 May | First A380 rear spar assembley delivered from Filton. |
| 2003 July | New 'West Factory' A380 wing manufacturing centre opened by Prime Minister, Tony Blair. |
| 2004 May | First A380 (flying) wing set delivered. |
| 2004 September | A380 fatigue test wing set delivered to the Hamburg test facility. |
| 2005 January | A380 wings seen in public for the first time at the 'Reveal' of the first complete aircraft in Toulouse. |
| 2005 April | A380 wings airborne for the fist time with the first flight of MSN 001 at Toulouse. |
| 2005 September | 4,000th Airbus wing set delivered. |
| 2007 August | Delivery of the 5,000th Broughton-built wing set. |
| 2013 September | Delivery of the first A350XWB carbon-fibre wing set. |

*Delivery for the loading of the 3,000th equipped single-aisle wing set wing from Broughton by Airbus A300-600ST Super Transporter 'Beluga' aircraft on 8 November 2006.*

Opposite: A major Airbus wing production milestone being appropriately celebrated in May 1992 with the hand-over of the 999th wing set, for an A340 for Lufthansa of Germany, in front of an undesignated A321. The 1,000th wing set, for an A310 for the Oasis Group of Spain and the 1,001st, for an A320 for Northwest Airlines of the USA, were also handed over in similar fashion at the same time. The whole triple celebration was held in the presence of a thousand members of the Chester workforce. they were arranged to emphasise visually the British Aerospace 'Arrow' corporate logo – thereby symbolising both the explosive growth of the Airbus family and its geographical market penetration, and justifying the contemporary and proudly proclaimed BAe slogan: 'Airbus – A Great British Success the World Over'.

# The Broughton Production Record

| Type | Time Period | No. Built |
|---|---|---|
| *Vickers-Armstrongs* | | |
| Wellington Mk.I | 1939 | 3 |
| Wellington Mk. IA | 1940 | 17 |
| Wellington Mk. IC | 1940-1942 | 1583 |
| Wellington Mk. III | 1941-1942 | 737 |
| Wellington Mk. IV | 1940-42 | 220 |
| Wellington Mk.X | 1942-1944 | 2434 |
| Wellington Mk.XII Tropicalised | 1943-1944 | 8 |
| Wellington Mk.XIV | 1943-1944 | 538 |
| Avro Lancaster B.Mk.1 | 1944-1945 | 235 |
| Avro Lincoln | 1945 | 11 |
| Total: | 1939-1945 | 5786 |
| | | |
| *de Havilland* | | |
| Mosquito T.F.37 and N.F.38 | 1948-1950 | 96 |
| Hornet N.F.21 | 1948-1952 | 149 |
| DHC Chipmunk | 1950-1956 | 889 |
| Vampire J.28B (Sweden) | 1949-1952 | 297 |
| Vampire F.B.Mk.5 | 1951-1952 | 87 |
| Vampire F.B.Mk.9 | 1950-1956 | 255 |
| Vampire N.F.Mk.10 | 1951-1952 | 55 |
| Vampire F.B.Mk.52 | 1950-1953 | 114 |
| Vampire N.F.Mk.54 | 1952-1953 | 12 |
| Vampire T.11 Trainer | 1952-1956 | 260 |
| Vampire T. 55 Export Trainer | 1955-1963 | 164 |
| Venom F.B.Mk.1 | 1952-1955 | 302 |
| Venom N.F.Mk.2 | 1952-1955 | 139 |
| Venom N.F.Mk.3 | 1955-1956 | 83 |
| Venom N.F.Mk.51/J.33 (Sweden) | 1952-1957 | 62 |
| Venom F.B.Mk.4 | 1955-1956 | 73 |
| Venom F.A.W.Mk.20 | 1954-1955 | 38 |
| Venom F.A.W.Mk.21 | 1955-1956 | 99 |
| Venom F.A.W.Mk.22 | 1956-1958 | 38 |
| Dove | 1951-1967 | 244 |
| Heron | 1953-1967 | 140 |
| Comet 2 | 1957 | 1* |
| Comet 4 | 1958-1964 | 40 |
| DHC Beaver | 1960-1967 | 46 |
| 125 | 1962-1963 | 4 |
| Sea Vixen | 1962-1966 | 30 |
| * Four others only partially completed | | |
| Total: | 1948-1966 | 2800 |
| | | |
| *Hawker Siddeley/British Aerospace/BAE Systems/Airbus UK* | | |
| 125 Series 1 700 | 1962-1985 | |
| Series 800 | 1983-1996 | |
| Series 1000 | 1990-1996 | |
| | | |
| Total: | 1962-1966 | 1086 |

TOTAL 'FLY-AWAY' AIRCRAFT BUILT    1939-1996                                         9672

Airbus Wing Sets:
*Hawker Siddeley/British Aerospace/BAE Systems/Airbus UK*

| | | |
|---|---|---|
| A300/A310 | 1971-2006 | 822 |
| A320/A321/A319/A318 | 1985-2014 | 6093 |
| A330/A340 | 1990-2014 | 1528 |
| A380 | 2004-2014 | 164 |
| A350XWB | 2012-2014 | 13 |

TOTAL AIRBUS WING SETS DELIVERED 1971 to 30 June 2014                   8620*
*Excluding a combined total of twelve test wings.


Other Work Programmes:
*Vickers-Armstrongs*

| | | |
|---|---|---|
| Pre-fabricated Houses | 1945-1948 | 11,250 |

*de Havilland*

| | | |
|---|---|---|
| Chipmunk, Dove and Heron overhauls | | |
| Royal Flight Heron servicing | | |
| RCAF Comet I modifications | 1956 | |
| Avro Shackleton overhauls | 1960-1962 | 24 |
| RAF Comet C2 strengthening | | |
| Vampire refurbishment | 1954-1964 | |

*Hawker Siddeley*

| | | |
|---|---|---|
| Vampire and Venom overhauls/resale | 1952-1971 | 1,271 |
| Trident component manufacture | 1960s | |
| Blackburn Beverley overhauls | 1962-1964 | 21 |
| Ex-BOAC Comet 4 modn for RAE | 1963 | 1 |
| Sea Vixen conversions | 1965-1968 | 37 |
| Nimrod Development prototypes | 1965 | 2 |
| Nimrod main airframe components | 1966-1970 | 41 |
| Hawker Hunter overhauls | 1971 | |
| HS748 final assembly | 1974-1975 | 2 |
| HS748 Coastguarder conversion | 1976 | 1 |

*British Aerospace/BAE Systems/Airbus UK*

| | | |
|---|---|---|
| Raytheon Hawker 800XP kits | 1996-2012 | 639 |

TOTAL 125 FLY-AWAY AIRCRAFT AND AIRFRAME KITS BUILT 1962-2012    1725

*Roll out of the first Airbus A320neo (new engine option) MSN6101 F-WNEO at Toulouse on 1 July 2014, with appropriately strengthened Broughton-built wings (now standard on all A320s) and fuel-saving sharklet wing-tips, prior to first service deliveries in 2015, and having already garnered more than 3,000 orders. Total A320 family orders now exceed 10,500.*

# Chronology of Key Broughton Events

| | |
|---|---|
| 1935 | British Government announces 'Shadow Factory' Scheme. |
| September 1936 | Decision taken to build and equip a new production factory for the Vickers Wellington. |
| 1938 | Decision taken for the Chester Factory to be Government-owned but leased to and managed by Vickers-Armstrongs. |
| 14 December 1938 | Ground-breaking and construction of Vickers-Chester Factory begins. |
| 3 April 1939 | Assembly of first Chester-built Wellington begins. |
| 2 August 1939 | First Chester-built Wellington airborne. |
| September 1939 | Vickers-Chester Factory fully operational. |
| 1941 | Cranage satellite opened. |
| September 1945 | Vickers-Chester/Cranage ceases Wellington production with the 5,540th aircraft. |
| June 1944 to August 1945 | Vickers-Chester produces 246 Avro Lancasters and Lincolns. |
| 1945–1948: | Vickers-Chester builds 11,250 prefabricated houses. |
| 1 July 1948 | Chester Factory formally taken over by de Havilland. |
| January 1960 | Chester Factory becomes part of Hawker Siddeley de Havilland Division. |
| 26 September 1967 | Hawker Siddeley Aviation (HSA) becomes British partner in emerging new European airliner programme and designates Chester as the wing manufacturing centre. |
| March 1969 | HSA keeps faith when British Government withdraws from European programme. |
| 29 May 1969 | Airbus Industrie (AI) A300 airliner programme launched. |
| 23 November 1971 | First completed A300 wing set dispatched from Chester |
| 1 January 1978 | Chester Factory becomes part of British Aerospace Hatfield-Chester Division. |
| 1 January 1979 | British Aerospace joins AI as full decision-making partner with 20 per cent shareholding and workshare. |
| 1 February 1989 Division | Chester becomes conjoined with Filton (Bristol) as the BAe Airbus of British Aerospace (Commercial Aircraft) Ltd. |
| April 1999 | British Aerospace Airbus receives the Queen's Award for Export Achievement 'in recognition of the significant contribution that the export of Airbus wings makes to the UK economy'. |
| 31 March 2000 | BAE Systems (formed on 30 November 1999) forms Airbus UK comprising Filton and Broughton. |
| 1 January 2001 | Airbus UK becomes part of the new autonomous Airbus integrated company with BAE Systems retaining a 20 per cent shareholding only in the new company. |
| August 2001 | Ground-breaking begins for the construction of the new 'West Factory'. |
| Early 2003 | Wales First Minister, Rhodri Morgan, opens 'East Factory' developments. |
| 4 July 2003 | Prime Minister Tony Blair opens the new A380 wing 'West Factory'. |
| 14 October 2006 | BAE Systems sells its 20 per cent shareholding in Airbus to the Franco-German-Spanish parent company, European Aeronautic Defence and Space company (EADS). |
| 13 October 2013 | Prime Minister David Cameron and Welsh First Minster Crwyn Lones, open new A350XWB wing 'North Factory'. |
| 2012 | Production of the Hawker 125 business jet ceased after 50 years of continuous production at Broughton. |
| 1 January 2014 | Broughton becomes part of the newly-designated Airbus Group (superceding the former EADS). |

# Enduring Broughton Heritage Tribute

The Avro Lancaster PA474 of the RAF Battle of Britain Memorial Flight (BBMF) is a vivid reminder of Vickers-Armstrongs' prodigious bomber production at the wartime Shadow Factory at Chester/Broughton. First built there in mid-1945, this historic aircraft is part of Broughton's rich seven-decade legacy to the heritage of Airbus UK of today. It is displayed annually throughout the United Kingdom, a deserving tribute to both the Broughton wartime output and its own classic status. The best known of 7,377 Lancasters built in the UK and Canada, 235 of which came from Broughton, PA474 is one of only two surviving airworthy examples in the world (the other is in Canada). Intended for service in the Far East, shortly after it entered service with 82 Squadron RAF at Benson, Oxfordshire, on 23 September 1948 wearing the individual letter 'M', the abrupt end of the war with Japan led to its assignment to photo reconnaissance duties in East and South Africa. It was then transferred to the College of Aeronautics at Cranfield, Bedfordshire, for flight trials with a Handley Page laminar-flow wing (mounted vertically above the rear fuselage) until 1964. Afterwards adopted by the Air Historical Branch (AHB), it appeared in two well-known films – *Operation Crossbow* and *The Guns of Navarone*. Taken back by the RAF at Waddington, Lincolnshire, in April 1964, it was given the markings of 44 Squadron's R5508 'KM-B', thereby reflecting the fact that this squadron became the first operational unit to receive the Lancaster in 1941 and commemorating John Nettleton VC and the aircraft that he flew on the Augsberg raid of 17 April 1942.

After restoration, the aircraft joined the BBMF in November 1973 and two years later was adopted by the City of Lincoln. In 1980, it was given the 'AJ-G' code of 617 Squadron's EE932, as flown by Wg. Cdr.Guy Gibson during the famous 'Dam Busters' raid of 16/17 May 1943, for the 1979 season. In 1984, it flew as 'SR-D' of 101 Squadron. After being contracted to West Country Air Services at Exeter, Devon, it returned to RAF Coningsby, Lincolnshire, and was given the 'PM-M²'code of ED888 which served 140 operations with 103 and 575 Squadrons. During the winter of 1995/96 it received a new main wing spar and the markings of W4964 'WS-J', Johnny Walker, an aircraft of 9 Squadron RAF which took part in the first attack on the German battleship Tirpitz. Undergoing a major overhaul at RAF St Athan, South Wales, in the winter of 1999/2000, the aircraft was again repainted, this time in the markings of 61 Squadron EE176 'QR-M' with the nose art 'Mickey the Moocher', Walt Disney's Mickey Mouse cartoon character. During the winter of 2006/7, PA474 underwent a complete 'back-to-bare-metal' overhaul and repaint for the first time with two different colour schemes and markings – on the port side as EE139 'Phantom of the Ruhr' coded HR-W of No.100 Squadron; and on the starboard side as BQ-B of No.550 Squadron. The aircraft notably appeared at the Imperial War Museum, Duxford, Cambridgeshire, in September 2007 for the celebration of 'Fifty Golden Years of the BBMF' (since the RAF's famous Historic Aircraft Flight was formed at Biggin Hill, Kent, in 1947). It now also represents one of Bomber Command's 'centenarians' – aircraft which took part in 100 or more wartime operations – and continues to lead the renowned BBMF displays operating from its home base at Coningsby.

# Acknowledgements

I have been immensely privileged to know and work with many of the Vickers-Weybridge people who originally set up both the Chester and Blackpool Shadow Factories, and many others during the de Havilland, Hawker Siddeley, British Aerospace, BAE Systems and Airbus UK tenures of the Chester/Broughton plant, and I must express my profound gratitude to them, and many thousands like them, for the magnificent story they have created, which continues happily in high activity, and that I have retold pictorially here.

To do so has required the help of many good friends and other willing supporters in loaning and providing appropriate photographs and information which I much appreciate. I am equally grateful to many of them for preserving this precious material in the first place, despite the many vicissitudes through which much of it has inevitable passed over the intervening 70 years.

In this respect, I am most grateful to my old Vickers friends Hugh Scrope, for his knowledge and records of the original Vickers-Armstrongs Shadow Factory, Bill Coomber for his first-hand recollections of his time during the early months of Chester, and the late Eric Morgan for the loan of the much-valued photos of its original construction and early operation – also to John Wells and Graham Waller for access to the Vickers PLC/Rolls-Royce archives now carefully preserved at the Cambridge University Library. I am likewise grateful to Ron Hedges, Barry Guess and Mike Fielding of BAE Systems Heritage at Farnborough. Also to Phil Jarrett, whose photographic collection has proved invaluable. Thanks also go to the late Barry Abraham for his expert historical knowledge of the Shadow Factories, the various airfields referred to and his many helpful comments – and his writings about them, together with Phil Butler, for Air-Britain Aeromilitaria and Airfield Review. Others who have been most helpful include Philip Birtles, the late Norman Boorer, Geoff Green, Harry Holmes, Derek Inskeep, Ian Lowe, the late Alec Lumsden and Sir Peter Masefield, Arthur Rowland, David Smith (especially in respect of his privately published book Hawarden – A Welsh Airfield 1939-79), Mike Stroud, Len Warrey, Michael Webb and his late father, Les, and colleagues at Brooklands Museum. I am also grateful to Christine Gregory of the RAF Museum, Hendon, Sandy Gilbert-Wykes at the Battle of Britain Memorial Flight, Derek Elliot at the Central Register for Air Photography at the National Assembly for Wales; Elizabeth Pettit at Flintshire County Council Records Office.

My special thanks go to the senior Airbus UK executives, Brian Fleet, for the insight of his inspirational leadership of the vast and invigorating Broughton operation of today, and to Iain Gray, Dr Gareth Williams, Henry Ashton and Frank Ogilvie for their highly informative technical papers on the A380 programme. I am also profoundly grateful to Mark Chaloner at Broughton for his consistently exceptional efforts, superb photography and ready response to my many requests and questions and without whom much of this book would not have been possible and to Phil McGraa for seeing this edition through to publication. Indeed, I have found a galvanizing ethos throughout Broughton that is reminiscent of the driving energy, pride and enthusiasm of the heyday of my own origins at Vickers-Weybridge, Broughton's original lineal parent. Grateful thanks also go to Howard Berry, Rob Bray, Tom Bright, Dave Charlton, Mike Fish and Barbara Ward at Airbus UK Filton; and to Francoise Tripiano at Airbus in Toulouse.

My old ex-British Aerospace friend, Mike Brown, now of Raytheon Systems Ltd in London, has also been most helpful – as has Julie Foster at BAE Systems Warton.

Lastly, I must express my fullest appreciation of the original inspiration and encouragement of my dear old friend, the late Jeffrey 'Monty' Montgomery, in tackling this intensely interesting and deserving subject, and together with his sister, the late Diana Amberton, for the first-hand memories of their time at Broughton with their parents during the extraordinarily challenging formative years of the Broughton saga.

Dr Norman Barfield 2014